BULLEID LOCOMOTIVES

Revised Edition

Cover:
'West Country' Pacifics No 34023 *Blackmore Vale* and rebuilt No 34108 *Wincanton* seen with the RCTS 'Farewell to Southern Steam' railtour at Upwey Wishing Well on 18 June 1967. *Brian Stephenson*

Previous page:
'West Country' class Pacific No 34038 *Lynton* slips violently as it starts the 18.30 Bournemouth train away from Waterloo on 6 June 1966; just two weeks before it was withdrawn from service. *M. S. Stokes*

Below:
Heading an up Kent Coast express, via Maidstone, 'Battle of Britain' class Pacific No 34073 *249 Squadron* was photographed in 1958, in BR Brunswick green livery. *A. C. Cawston*

BULLEID LOCOMOTIVES
Revised Edition
Brian Haresnape

LONDON
IAN ALLAN LTD

First published 1977
Reprinted 1979
Revised edition 1985
Reprinted 1993

ISBN 0 7110 1539 2

Published by Ian Allan Ltd, Shepperton, Surrey; and printed by Ian Allan Printing Ltd at its works at Coombelands in Runnymede, England.

For my late Mother, who encouraged my boyhood enthusiasm for steam locomotives

Below:
'Merchant Navy' class Pacific No 35015 *Rotterdam Lloyd* is seen leaving Waterloo sometime in the 1949/50 period when this class was painted in standard blue livery, with black and white lining. The colour did not wear well and was soon replaced by the Brunswick green. *British Rail*

Below right:
'West Country' class Pacific No 21C116 *Bodmin* struggles for adhesion as it commences banking the up 'Devon Belle' Pullman Car train out of Ilfracombe in August 1947; with a Pullman observation car attached to the rear of the train. The steam operated sanding gear is in use. *C. A. Todhunter*

Contents

Foreword

All fascinating subjects repay detailed examination and there are many veins of intricate detail in the huge arena of steam locomotives. But often a step back from detail is rewarding, to picture as a whole the locomotives of one type, or one railway, or one designer. Then one gets a grand impression of the general scene, as of the Bulleid engines so admirably presented in this pictorial history.

Though ready to improve the smallest detail, O. V. S. Bulleid was himself very keen on a clear view of the general scene. He liked those pictorial mile-by-mile descriptions of railway routes, and illustrated features as in *Country Life,* and he would have liked to see pictorial histories of anyone's steam locomotives, not least his own.

Steam engines are like the best sculptures of human and animal figures. In them one recognizes brain, body and limbs. By the pose one tells their work or intent. But the steam engine can go into action, leaving the sculpture standing. Here specially a pictorial history scores by presenting these attractive iron horses as they go about their wide-ranging duties.

This pictorial history displays the Bulleid locomotives in all moods, from repose to demonaic energy. It gives a grand parade of a fine stud of engines.

H. A. V. Bulleid.

Introduction

No one, it seems, was more surprised than Bulleid himself when, in May 1937, he was sent for by Sir Herbert Walker, the Chairman of the Southern Railway, and told that he could have the job of CME of the Southern if he would apply for it. The retiring Chief Mechanical Engineer, R. E. L. Maunsell, stayed on during the September in which Bulleid settled in, and on 1 October 1937 Bulleid took over completely.

Prior to this unexpected change, Bulleid had been Assistant to Nigel Gresley, the CME of the LNER, and had been absorbed in technical and experimental work for many years, being closely involved with all the many Gresley triumphs and achievements. Suddenly he found himself the "Chief" and confronted with a railway which in recent years had devoted more time, energy and money to electric traction than to steam. The results of Bulleid's transformation of Southern steam power between the immediate pre-World War 2 days and the nationalisation of the railways in 1948 forms the larger part of the contents of this pictorial history.

Born in New Zealand on 19 September 1882 of British parents, O. V. S. Bulleid came to Britain in 1889 upon the death of his father. His childhood and early teens were spent in Accrington living with relatives and he then obtained a four-year premium apprenticeship under H. A. Ivatt at the Doncaster works of the Great Northern Railway, commencing on 21 January, 1901. By January 1907 he had become Assistant to the Locomotive Works Manager. But Bulleid was ambitious and at this point he succeeded in obtaining a job in France; he left the GNR in December, to become the Assistant Works Manager and Chief Draughtsman of the French Westinghouse Company, at their Freinville works near Paris. Next he obtained the post of Mechanical Engineer to the Exhibitions Branch of the Board of Trade, for the Brussels (1910) and Turin (1911) Exhibitions.

In December 1911, with his latest job at an end, Bulleid (by now a married man of 29 with a year-old daughter) returned to Doncaster and sought to rejoin the GNR. He became Personal Assistant to Gresley, who was then taking over

Above:
Maunsell 'Lord Nelson' class 4-6-0 No 863 *Lord Rodney* alongside Bulleid 'Battle of Britain' class 4-6-2 No 21C160 (then unnamed) at Waterloo on 20 March 1948. The Maunsell engine has the improved front end, with multiple-jet blastpipe and large diameter chimney, which was one of Bulleid's first design improvements following his appointment as Chief Mechanical Engineer of the Southern Railway. He made similar modifications to other classes of Maunsell locomotive, including a few 'King Arthurs'. *C. C. B. Herbert*

Left:
Bulleid-Firth-Brown (BFB) disc centre wheels on a 'Battle of Britain' Pacific; also showing the slide bar cover which was applied to some engines in an attempt to prevent sand from the leading sandpipe reaching the motion. The cylinder cocks, with rodding and the clasp brake gear, are also well illustrated. *Ian Allan Library*

7

as Locomotive, Carriage & Wagon Superinten-
dent. Thus began their close association which
spanned more than a quarter of a century, in-
terrupted for Bulleid only by four years of war
service from 1915 to 1919. With the formation
of the London & North Eastern Railway,
Gresley became CME and Bulleid was
appointed as his assistant, with offices in
London, in the early months of 1923. Bulleid's
activities, which ranged widely from carriage
and wagon design to locomotive testing and
technical experiments of many kinds, are
outside the scope of the present volume, which
is only concerned with the locomotives
designed by him after leaving the LNER.
Nevertheless, it is clear that many of his ex-
periences working alongside Gresley were to
colour his attitudes in later years.

In retrospect, Bulleid was a born inventor
and one, moreover, with an insatiable appetite
for trying out his ideas in practice. He loved
visiting outside firms to see their methods and
ideas, and particularly in his later years (when
concerned with the dieselisation of the Irish
National Rail system) he took delight in the
design alternatives that were tendered by
outside contractors. Whilst working with
Gresley he succeeded in getting a number of his

Above:
Bulleid was impressed by the performance of the
Maunsell 'Schools' class 4-4-0s, but nevertheless
included them in his programme for improved front
ends, with a multiple-jet blastpipe. Not all the engines
of the class were dealt with, as the improvement was
marginal. A further experiment was made with No 937
Epsom in 1939, when Bulleid extended the smokebox
and set the blastpipe at an angle to the vertical;
housed in a particularly ugly stovepipe chimney. The
scheme was soon discarded. *J. P. Wilson*

Above right:
An impressive angle to view a 'Merchant Navy' as No
35028 leans to the curve through Clapham Junction
with the down 6.30pm Waterloo to Bournemouth
express on 27 June 1949. The nameplates are boarded
over, pending the official naming ceremony. The
profile of the tender matched the postwar Bulleid
passenger stock. *C. C. B. Herbert*

Right:
Memories of summer holidays in the past, with
Malachite green engines in lush West Country
landscapes, are evoked by 'West Country' class Pacific
No 34019 *Bideford* heading an Exeter-Plymouth local
at Dainton, WR, with a train of ex-LMS stock, still in
maroon livery. *J. G. Hubback*

Right:
Excusing the crude appearance of his wartime 'Q1' class 'austerity' 0-6-0 goods engine, Bulleid was quick to observe that 'form follows function'. He certainly broke away completely from the classic conventions of British steam locomotive design! This comparison of front ends, taken at Reading South shed on 20 April 1956, surely speaks for itself. The locomotive in the background is an ex SECR 4-4-0; one of Wainwright's very graceful 'D' class. *R. C. Riley*

Below:
Another contrast of styles, this time at Eastleigh on 12 May 1962, with the preserved exLSWR Drummond Class T9 4-4-0 No 120 in the background. It could be argued that the plain stovepipe chimney on the 'T9' (a latterday alteration by Urie,) foreshadowed things to come! The lack of splashers to the coupled wheels was a particularly stark feature of Bulleid's 0-6-0s; No 33023 is pictured here. *M. Pope*

Bottom left:
Somehow the bleak winter weather seems to emphasise the stark outline of the Bulleid 'Q1', No 33006, which is seen here heading a Reading-Redhill passenger train near Betchworth on 28 December 1964. *Brian Stephenson*

Top:
One of the most controversial steam locomotives ever designed, the unique 'Leader' class 0-6-6-0T was Bulleid's last design for the Southern Railway and in fact did not appear until after nationalisation. One of the least satisfactory aspects proved to be the fireman's compartment, which became unbearably hot. The fireman is visible, leaning well out of the cab and with the door part-open in this view of No 36001 on a trial run near Lewes. Oil-firing (as originally intended by Bulleid) would have reduced the problem to some extent. *Author's collection*

pet schemes tried out and subsequently adopted, sometimes getting his knuckles rapped by his Chief in the process!

One locomotive of the Gresley era, in particular, seems to have a bearing on what followed on the Southern. This was the magnificent 2-8-2 passenger engine *Cock o' the North,* intended for the heavy trains and difficult grades of the Edinburgh-Aberdeen line. Bulleid and Gresley worked in close accord on the design of this engine and in it one may see the genesis of Bulleid's later Pacifics. In fact, at one stage he considered a 2-8-2 design for the SR duties which the 'Merchant Navy' Pacifics eventually undertook. Externally *Cock o' the North* had unusual lines for a British locomotive, and the front end arrangement with sloping top to the smokebox and integral smoke deflectors carried forward from the boiler casing were features to be seen in modified form on No 21C1 *Channel Packet* in her original condition.

One of Bulleid's first actions on arrival at Waterloo was personally to test the existing main-line motive power, by making footplate runs. An early result was the provision of improved front end and exhaust for the Maunsell 'Lord Nelson' class, also for some of the 'Schools' and a handful of 'King Arthurs'. Unfortunately whilst the multiple-jet Lemaître exhaust used by Bulleid certainly invigorated the locomotives concerned it did nothing for their appearance!

11

Right:
Perhaps the genesis of the Bulleid Pacific front-end may be seen in Gresley's Class P2 2-8-2 No 2001 *Cock o' the North* with the sloping top to the smokebox and the smoke deflectors incorporated into the boiler casing. Bulleid was closely involved in the design and testing of this engine, whilst on the LNER. *British Rail*

Below:
Drifting exhaust has momentarily completely obscured the driver's vision as a blustery wind beats against 'Merchant Navy' Pacific No 35014 *Nederland Line,* seen near Basingstoke on 8 September, 1952. This was a constant problem with the air-smoothed casing of the Bulleid engines, partly due to the prevailing south-west winds of the region in which they operated and partly inherent in the front-end design. Many attempts were made to overcome this feature, without any great success. *Roy E. Wilson*

Below right:
A handsome transformation. The removal of Bulleid's air-smoothed casing and the application of Walschaerts valve gear when the engines were modified by British Railways (as described in Part Two on pages 78-89) produced a locomotive of impressive appearance, not unlike the larger BR standard designs. No 35023 *Holland-Afrika Line* was photographed at Southampton Central on 2 March 1957. The tender was the last to receive from Eastleigh works the old-style BR lion-and-wheel emblem. *G. Wheeler*

A report on the state of the existing steam stock, plus Bulleid's powers of persuasion, resulted in Southern Railway agreement to a steam locomotive modernisation scheme. First on the list was what was described as a fast mixed-traffic locomotive. This was envisaged as a 4–8–2 capable of good acceleration, a top speed sufficient for 75 mph bookings and good route availability for both passenger and freight workings. Turntable limitations forced the reduction of overall length to a 2–8–2 wheel arrangement, which produced hostile reactions from the Civil Engineer, until a Helmholtz pony truck was proposed; then Bulleid did, in fact, get agreement for two 2–8–2s to be built for trials. He nevertheless foresaw problems in gaining acceptance, and proposed a 4–6–2 alternative, which was more readily agreed upon. The resulting 'Merchant Navy' Pacific is described on pages 18–35.

In retrospect it seems that Bulleid was always the victim of time. He arrived on the Southern just as the winds of war were beginning to unsettle the nation. By the time his first locomotive was ready Britain was in the darkest days of World War 2. His second locomotive design, the ugly Q1 0–6–0, was essentially an engine of war, produced for a specific and urgent need. Towards the end of the war it was possible to plan for peacetime and the Light Pacifics emerged in quantity in the immediate post-war months. But already another change was on the horizon, in the form of the impending nationalisation of the railways, and Bulleid was approaching retirement age as he worked on the design of his highly unconventional 'Leader' class. Even in Ireland, where he went after leaving the Southern, his 'Turf Burner' was produced at the eleventh hour of steam, and was overtaken by a decision to dieselise the entire CIE system.

A very considerable amount has been written both for and against the Bulleid locomotives. There is no doubt that some of the more unconventional features he introduced did not prove satisfactlory in everyday service, and the operating department viewed them with considerable dislike, in particular the chain-driven valve gear of the Pacifics and the oil-bath which encased it. The engines steamed well, in particular the superb boilers on the Pacifics, but they were heavy on coal and oil. They showed a fine turn of speed on many occasions but their day-to-day availability was not high by existing standards. They were unpredictable, and their behaviour ranged from magnificent to downright unpleasant from the enginemen's viewpoint. A recently shopped Pacific would sparkle in its performance, delighting train recorders with their stopwatches, but at high cost.

Personally I have a great affection for them, as I lived near the West of England main line when the Pacifics were in their heyday. The Malachite green livery suited their odd exterior very well and they looked good at the head of a train of Bulleid's admirable post-war carriages. Many pleasant memories are revived of summer holiday excursions to the "Strong Country" when I see pictures of the engines in this state. I well recall the shock of seeing No. 35024 pounding through Wimbledon station in ex-works condition, in an experimental blue livery which was quickly adopted for the rest of the class. It looked quite smart on the air-smoothed casing, but (except for Pullmans) it clashed badly with the colour of the rolling stock. I could never raise much enthusiasm for their final livery of dark green, which seemed so unsuitable to their form when compared to Bulleid's original scheme.

It is not my intention to enter the debate on the pros and cons of Bulleid's engines in any detail, as a number of learned writers have already added much fuel to the fire in recent years, and no doubt there is more to come. My present work is presented to the reader as a straightforward pictorial survey of the various Bulleid engines in the many stages of their careers from delivery to withdrawal. As far as possible I have included the various detail alterations which took place over the years and I have used illustrations to emphasise these

Below:
Equally successful was the appearance of the rebuilt Light Pacifics, as is well illustrated in this lovely view of 'Battle of Britain' Pacific No 34088 *213 Squadron* working the down 'Golden Arrow'. The train has just emerged from Knockholt Tunnel. *Derek Cross*

Right:
Once familiar sight as the crew prepared for the road. The fireman climbs to the footplate of rebuilt 'Battle of Britain' Pacific No 34087 *145 Squadron* at Weymouth shed. The engine was booked to work the Channel Islands Boat Train. *M. J. Esau*

points, which may be of particular help to railway modellers.

The book is divided into two main parts, the first dealing with Bulleid's designs for the Southern and for the CIE. The second part deals with the modification to the Pacifics undertaken by British Railways after Bulleid had left. Added to this are appendices dealing with diesel and electric locomotives, named locomotives and preserved examples. I would have liked to have added a further section, dealing with Bulleid's contribution to passenger carriage design, as this was an aspect of his work which produced some remarkable results. When I wrote these words (1975) the SR still relied heavily upon suburban electric stock dating from the Bulleid era – which surely must have paid for itself again and again since built.

I have already mentioned the move that Bulleid made from British Railways to the Irish National Rail system. This was in October 1949. Prior to this he had been involved with the Milne Report of 1948, which had examined the state of rail, road and canal transport in Eire for which Bulleid had been technical assessor.

Nearly seventy years of age and with no prospect for the continuation of his designs on the nationalised railways in Britain, O. V. S. Bulleid became Consulting Mechanical Engineer of CIE, and by February 1951 he had become CME, a position he held until May 1958 when he retired. This final phase of his railway career saw him as active as ever, as he modernised the CME's department and masterminded the changeover from steam to diesel traction.

In the pages that follow each of the Bulleid designs is dealt with in chronological order. It will be seen that his actual output was relatively small, when compared to the large numbers of locomotives of – for example – Stanier or Churchward. Whilst this is true, it must be acknowledged that Bulleid's contribution to the story of the British steam locomotive was exceptional. He took the classic Stephenson concept and attempted to improve upon it in a multitude of ways; if he failed in some cases this was as much the result of frustrations due to prevailing conditions (i.e. the outbreak of war or the nationalisation of the Southern Railway) as it was to technical inadequacy. In a nutshell,

Bulleid lived through the eleventh hour of British steam. The end was inevitable, but he did much to enliven the last of steam whilst the birth pangs of dieselisation were forced upon his reluctant attention.

This revised edition has a number of new illustrations and an additional Appendix dealing with the preserved Bulleid locomotives, and I am grateful to Alan Butcher of Ian Allan Ltd for providing an up-to-date list of their whereabouts. I would like, once more, to thank in particular my dear friend Alec Swain for his constant assistance, also the many people who heeded my original request for pictures and information and in particular I would like to thank the following: Colin Boocock; H. C. Casserley; L. Elsey; A. B. MacLeod; S. C. Nash; D. Piper; N. E. Preedy; Peter Rowledge and S. C. Townroe. The line drawings include two specially drawn by Peter Winding, who also gave much assistance on the choice of illustrations; other line drawings are reproduced by courtesy of the *Railway Gazette* and Ian Allan Library.

Brian Haresnape FRSA NDD
Ramatuelle, France
September 1984

Above left:
The camera captures the blurred driving wheels of rebuilt 'Battle of Britain' class 4-6-2 No 34089 *602 Squadron* as the locomotive momentarily loses adhesion, leaving Waterloo with a train for Weymouth. *M. J. Esau*

Above:
Steam departure. Rebuilt 'West Country' Pacific No 34018 *Axminster* makes a pleasing picture pulling out of Basingstoke with a Bournemouth train on 28 November 1964. *J. B. Wells*

Bulleid Steam

New locomotives introduced by O. V. S. Bulleid for the Southern Railway and the CIE from 1941 to 1957, including his experimental 'Leader' class 0-6-6-0T for the Southern and its turf-burning counterpart in Ireland. The subsequent BR rebuilds of the Pacifics are described on pages 78 - 97.

4–6–2 Class MN (BR power class 8P*) Express Passenger Engines

Introduced: 1941
Total: 30
'Merchant Navy'

*Originally given as 7P

It was in March 1938 that the Southern Railway Board's authority was given for the construction of 10 new main-line steam locomotives of a new and, as yet undefined, design. Bulleid had outlined his task as the production of a locomotive capable of hauling trains of 550-600 tons at start-to-stop average speeds of 60 mph (on the Continental boat trains) and 70 mph (on the Western Section). As mentioned in the introduction he at first considered locomotives with eight-coupled driving wheels, but he finally settled for the 4–6–2 wheel arrangement, following objections from the Civil Engineer. If anyone at the time

Below:
The drawing shows the original version of the 'Merchant Navy' class, with estimated weights, issued in 1941. The water filler for the tender is shown at the cab end, a feature later abandoned.

Bottom:
Diagram issued in 1945, showing front end modifications and altered weights. It was only applicable to a few engines attached to the original tender design.

anticipated a Gresley-inspired Pacific adapted to Southern Railway requirements, their guess was to prove remarkably wide of the mark. Bulleid set about producing a totally new design, with a number of quite novel aspects. In the course of time he showed himself capable of changing his mind – right up to the last minutes of design and construction – giving the drawing office staff a hectic time.

The outbreak of World War 2 overtook Bulleid in the midst of work on the first of the new engines, which did not appear until the early weeks of 1941. With a most unorthodox appearance, described as air-smoothed, (and intended to allow cleaning through carriage-washing plants) the new Pacific could hardly have been born at a more inopportune time.

Basically, the engine was a three-cylinder simple, with a novel chain-driven three-throw crank shaft operating valve gears for each cylinder and with an oil-bath totally enclosing the sets of motion, located between the frames. Added to this breakaway from established practice was a whole host of new items, including patent Bulleid-Firth-Brown type wheels; clasp-type brakes; a boiler pressure of 280lb psi, welded steel firebox and thermic syphons. A wealth of labour-saving features ensured a ready welcome from railway shed

Above:

The first 'Merchant Navy' engine, completed at Eastleigh in February 1941 and illustrated in as-built condition. The position of the numberplate and electric lights on the front end, above the bufferbeam, was quickly altered. The air-smoothed side casing was carried over the top and brought to a peak above the smokebox, with an air slot below. Livery was a matt finish Malachite green, with broad yellow lines, and the large brass castings used for name, number and ownership plates on both engine and tender had a red background. Wheel centres were also green, whilst the roof above the guttering was finished in matt black. A pivoting flat cap was provided on the roof to cover the chimney when the engine was 'cold', and the rear of the cab and tender front was roofed over, with flexible rubber bellows linking the two. The top of the casing on No 21C1 *Channel Packet* had a flat depression around the chimney area. The air intake to the chimney from the vertical front of the smokebox proved ineffective as a smoke-and-steam raiser. No 21C1 worked a 20-coach test train from Eastleigh to Bournemouth and back on 22 February 1941 and was named *Channel Packet* at Eastleigh on 10 March 1941 by Lt-Col J.T.C. Moore-Brabazon, the Minister of Transport. *Author's collection*

19

Left:
Front-end of No 21C1 *Channel Packet* in as-built condition,with front footstep on left-hand buffer only. Large cast brass ownership and number plates. Air intake above smokebox door, leading to the chimney. *Ian Allan Library*

Top:
By June 1941, the teething troubles with No 21C1 had mounted to a stage where the engine was often seen on freight workings, a pattern which continued during 1942-3 with the rest of the first batch of ten engines, whilst efforts were made to eradicate the troubles. These troubles included excess weight and poor smoke clearance. Early detail modifications to the pioneer engine, seen here, included re-positioning of the front numberplate and electric lights, and provision of inset footholds on the sloping front below the smokebox. An order was issued that the class should be kept west of Salisbury until they were more satisfactory performers, and three of the Eastleigh design staff were sent to watch over them. There was persistent trouble with broken rocking-shafts and

problems with the steel firebox, which developed a tendency to crack. Two ex-LSWR locomotives, an 'A12' class 0-4-2 No 646 and an 'X6' class 4-4-0 No 657, were specially adapted to supply steam to Nos 21C1/2 whilst on shed, as it was intended to keep the Pacifics constantly in steam. At first there was one engine at Exmouth Junction and one at Salisbury; later both were at Salisbury.   *Ian Allan Library*

Above:
The second 'Merchant Navy', No 21C2 *Union Castle,* was completed at Eastleigh in June 1941. A noticeable modification was the enlarged air intake above the smokebox door, which exposed the flat sloping top of the smokebox (a feature of No 21C1 also, but one which was concealed by the casing). This was applied to the remaining eight engines of the original batch, but still did not prove sufficient. The casing between the bufferbeam and front of the cylinders was cut away to expose the leading bogie wheel and there was a footstep and block on both buffers. Despite weight problems the large cast brass plates were retained. *British Rail*

21

Left:
Large painted number on the front, and additional date of building on the smokebox door plate, which no longer resembles the inverted horseshoe. Square hole round the chimney, with enlarged front slot. No 21C3 *Royal Mail* was photographed at Eastleigh on 21 October 1941, in the matt paint finish. Excess weight for the first two engines led to the decision not to fit the large metal numberplates to No 21C3, although these were in fact manufactured. To reduce the weight of Nos 21C1-5 holes were bored in the frames, and for Nos 21C6 onward lighter frames were constructed. *Ian Allan Library*

Above left:
This view of No 21C2 *Union Castle* making a rare visit to the Brighton line with a four-coach special at Merstham in July 1941, clearly shows the cut-away portion above the smokebox, exposing the multiple-jet chimney casing, which has a square hole surrounding it. On the return run the locomotive's valve gear failed at Streatham Common and the ensemble was hauled ignominiously by an exLBSCR 'I3' class 4-4-2T for the remainder of the journey! *Author's collection*

Left:
Superstition among enginemen associated with the 'Merchant Navy' engines led to the alteration of the smokebox door ownership plate. Originally this resembled an inverted horseshoe (see previous illustrations of Nos 21C1/2), which was changed to a complete circle, with the place and date of building added below the word 'Southern' No 21C3 *Royal Mail* displays this modification, together with the more serious abandonment of the cast brass numberplates and ownership plates on engine and tender – a move made to reduce weight. The main frames had lightening holes cut into them away from the stress areas. No 21C3 was delivered from Eastleigh in September 1941 and was named at Waterloo on 24 October 1941. The tender water filler is visible in this illustration. *Ian Allan Library*

staff, hard-pressed by the wartime conditions under which they then operated – until things began to go wrong.

The boiler was a magnificent affair, but it weighed too much (as did the valve motion) and economies had to be made in other parts to keep locomotive weight down to permissible levels. The boiler pressure was the highest that had ever been used in a British locomotive (other than in certain experimental designs). The boilers for the first 10 locomotives were built by the North British Locomotive Company, in Glasgow, as that famous firm had already considerable experience in the building of welded steel fireboxes – a feature chosen by Bulleid to reduce weight. The boiler barrel was tapered on the underside only and had a heating surface of 2176sq ft. The firebox (with combustion chamber) had 275sq ft including syphons, making a total evaporative surface of 2451sq ft. The superheater heating surface was 822sq ft, and the grate area of the wide firebox was $48\frac{1}{2}$sq ft. A multi-jet blast-pipe was fitted. In service these boilers proved to be magnificent steam producers.

The three cylinders were 18in diameter by 24in stroke, with the inside cylinder set at the very steep inclination of 1 in $7\frac{1}{2}$. With the intention of reducing the everyday maintenance routine of shed staff, Bulleid introduced his oil bath, which totally enclosed the valve motion, and which was meant to eliminate attention to the lubrication of the motion whilst the engine ran its entire span of service between works

Above:
Wartime black livery for No 21C5 *Canadian Pacific*, photographed at Eastleigh Works in March 1942. The locomotive was officially named at a ceremony held at Victoria Station, on 27 March 1942, by Mr F.W. Mottley of the Canadian Pacific Railway Company, one of a number or such ceremonies held for the new engines, despite the stringent wartime attitudes then prevailing. From No 21C3 onward the cut away at the leading end of the tender sides was reduced in an effort to improve cab comfort. No 21C4 *Cunard White Star* was shot up by a German aircraft near Whimple in November 1942. The crew escaped injury and the engine was quickly repaired and returned to service. *Ian Allan Library*

Right:
Minor changes were made in attempts to improve smoke deflection, with little or no effect, and in a determined effort to improve matters Bulleid placed the problem with Southampton University. A wooden scale model of a 'Merchant Navy' was constructed at Lancing Carriage works and sent to the University's wind tunnel. As a result of these experiments, in which the flow of air was studied, the front end of No 21C10 *Blue Star* was modified as shown. Similar modifications were made to Nos 21C8/9. The casing above the smokebox was brought forward in a lip, or cowl, and the sides were cut into to form individual side wings. A considerable improvement was observed in tests using a ciné camera located behind the driver's cab front window, although the design was criticised because it further restricted the view forward. A compromise solution was reached, with the top cowling separate from the side deflectors, which were flattened to reduce the overall width at the smokebox end. *Ian Allan Library*

overhauls. This oil bath had a capacity of no less than 40 gallons and included reversible gear pumps, chain driven from the valve crankshaft, to lift oil from the sump through pipes, and distribute it over the moving parts. It proved impossible to prevent leakage of oil and in some cases outbreaks of fire occurred when the oil soaked into the boiler lagging.

The design of the valve gear itself was to allow for this total enclosure in the oil bath, set between the main frames. The space available was relatively small. Bulleid's intention was to create a locomotive with its parts running in oil — like his car. This scheme was drawn-up before the war using a chain drive, without conventional valve spindles. Quite late in the day he considered using an improved Caprotti gear, but perhaps Bulleid foresaw the problems of

wartime production, as it was the patent chain-driven radial gear which he finally adopted for his new Pacifics. He fitted a steam-operated reverser, and it was the poor performance of this latter feature, together with the valve gear, which was to cause so much trouble in everyday service, until the modifications made by BR eliminated both causes (see pages 78-89.)

The spacing of the frames was closer than normal, with the centres of the horn cheeks in line with them. The first two engines were too heavy and holes were cut, in the frames, to lighten them; later engines of the first batch of 10 had these alterations from new. The massive cast steel frame stretchers were also reduced in weight as much as possible. Another method of reducing the overall weight of the locomotives (which had proved to be 90.15

Above:
No 21C16, delivered in March 1945 in austere black livery and seen here working a down West of England express near Hook. The second batch of engines Nos 21C11-20, were delivered between December 1944 and June 1945 in preparation for peacetime and had numerous detail changes compared to the initial 10. As built, they had short, flat smoke deflectors, set at a slope, and the front-end side valances were shortened, with a modified inward curve to the bufferbeam. The cutaway to expose the coupled wheels was more

angular and there were modifications to the cab and tender contours. The side sheets of the cab were turned inwards to give added protection to the crew, and windows were let into them. The tender side sheets were similarly treated, and a 'tunnel' ran between the coal space and the tender sides, giving the crew a better rearward vision, also providing housing for the fireirons. The middle lamp irons were relocated, on the smokebox door, instead of on the inside front edge of the smoke deflectors.
M. W. Earley

Right:

The pioneer Bulleid Pacific, No 21C1 *Channel Packet* was selected to work the inaugural trip of the 'Golden Arrow' Pullman train, when it was restored on 13 April 1946 with the return to peacetime conditions. In the latter days of World War 2 the locomotive had run in plain black livery, but had retained the cast brass name and number plates – somewhat surprisingly – and these plates remained when Eastleigh outshopped No 21C1 in full Malachite green livery – certainly a sight for sore eyes after the drab war years. The front end had an interim modification, following the experiments with No 21C10; the side casing was pressed out to form small deflectors with a cowl above the smokebox on which the top electric light was located. A footstep was added to the right-hand buffer, but the curved cowling was retained between bufferbeam and cylinders. The effect of a glossy varnish finish to the livery makes an interesting comparison with the original matt finish applied to Nos 21C1-3 when new (see pages 19-22).
Ian Allan Library

Above:

This view of No 21C8 *Orient Line* taken at Eastleigh Works in August 1947 shows a further alteration to the original design of the front end; now with smoke deflectors more apparent. A new style of cab, with raked-back front windows has also been fitted. The engine is in full gloss Malachite green livery, with yellow lining bands, and also has Malachite green coupled and leading bogie wheels. *L. Elsey*

Above right:

Poor quality coal probably contributed to this magnificent smoke effect as 'Merchant Navy' Pacific *Nederland Line* raises steam prior to departure from Bournemouth Central on an up express, c1947. The short smoke deflectors and more angular style of the external casing makes an interesting comparison with the two preceding photos. The tender was of 5,100 gal capacity, with modified springing. *G. Cunningham*

Right:

Four 'Merchant Navy' Pacifics were selected to take part in the historic Exchange Trials of 1948. These were Nos 35017-35020 (formerly Nos 21C17-21C20) and for these trials at least two were temporarily attached to LMSR Stanier tenders, (fitted with water scoops), which were unfortunately painted plain black, whereas the engines were in Malachite green with yellow lining. No 35020 was held in reserve on the Southern and was not in fact used. Two locomotives put up some terrific performances during the trials, No 35017 which ran on the London Midland and Eastern Regions, and No 35019 which ran on the Western. For trials on the Southern's homeground, No 35018 was selected, attached to its normal tender. Pictured here is No 35019 *French Line CGT* in Sonning Cutting during the WR trials, with a down Plymouth express on 27 April 1948; the ex-GWR Dynamometer Car is immediately behind the Stanier tender.
M. W. Earley

tons empty) was the use of thinner sheeting for the air-smoothed casing and the cab sides. The empty weight was reduced to 86.55tons, or 96.3tons in full working order. The ornamental cast brass numberplates on cabsides and front and the large cast 'Southern' plates on the tender were also removed, to reduce weight, and were replaced by painted letters and numerals.

The BFB (Bulleid-Firth-Brown) wheels were a patent variation on the box type, and had the advantage of greater and more continuous support for the tyre. The coupled wheel diameter was 6ft 2in, the leading bogie was 3ft 1in and the trailing axle had 3ft 7in diameter wheels. This latter axle was carried by a trailing truck of the 'delta' type. No reciprocating balance weights were used for the coupled driving wheels, but weights were inserted in the wheel rims in respect of rotating weights.

A considerable amount of attention was given by Bulleid to providing greater comfort and ease of operation, from the enginemen's viewpoint. In particular he provided electric lighting, worked from a steam generator. This illuminated the headcode lamps at the front of the engine and the rear of the tender, inspection

Above right:

Prior to naming, with the nameplates boarded over, No 35028 (later *Clan Line*) dusts the countryside near Pirbright Junction, hauling the 3.20 pm down Bournemouth express on 8 October 1949. The engine is in lined Malachite green, but has no emblem or lettering on the tender. The tender is the enlarged 6,000 gal version, which weighed 53.5 tons in full working order, and had a wheelbase of 14ft 4in compared to 13ft for the original design. This final batch of 10 locomotives was delivered new with the modified cab and with TIA water treatment equipment. *G. J. Jefferson*

Right:

The light blue livery, with black and white lining, as applied to No 35027 *Port Line*, made a colourful contrast to the traditional Pullman car umber and cream. The 10.00 am 'Golden Arrow' is seen here leaving Victoria in fine-style on 3 April 1950. The blue livery was relatively short-lived, as it did not wear well in service, but it graced the Bulleid engines more happily than the later dark green, although the original Malachite scheme was probably the most effective the Pacifics ever carried in original form. *B. Canning*

An American-type Berkely stoker was fitted to No 21C5 *Canadian Pacific* in March 1948. The mechanical stoker consisted of a coal crusher and conveying screws, which delivered coal from the tender to a distributor plate fitted in the firehole door. The progress of this particular locomotive on the Waterloo-Surbiton stretch was a sore point with householders on the lineside, as the engine frequently left a huge pall of black smoke hanging in the air for minutes after the train had passed! This engine was also highly unpopular with dining car staff and Pullman stewards as the coal dust penetrated the interior and soiled the white table linen. The locomotive's tender was adapted to carry a coal pusher and the small steam engine which drove the feeding screws, and the ashpan was slightly modified. In BR passenger blue livery, and renumbered 35005. *Canadian Pacific* is seen here at Clapham Junction, attached to the LMR Mobile Test Unit, during trials between Waterloo and Salisbury. Prior to this the engine was tried on the Rugby test plant, in March 1950.   *Ian Allan Library*

lights under the casing and above the wheels, and also the cab interior and fittings; a light below the footplate allowed the fireman to check the working of the injectors at night. The layout of the cab was revised from previous SR practice and the grouping of controls for both driver and fireman was altered to allow both men to perform their duties without getting in each other's way. Steam-operated firedoors were fitted, as in contemporary American practice.

The six-wheeled tender was of welded construction and the profile of the sides matched that of the post-war Bulleid carriages. The first tender had an array of footsteps and grab handles on the rear, later replaced by tubular steel ladders, and there were tank fillers on each side at the cab end, as well as in the normal position on top at the back. Water capacity was 5000gal and coal capacity 5tons for the first 10 tenders, which weighed 50tons in working order.

Right:
A bizarre combination of blue-liveried tender coupled to green-liveried engine, seen on No 35002 *Union Castle* at Nine Elms shed on 22 March 1952. The engine still had the original cab design although the front end had been up-dated with smoke deflectors and trough. The tender illustrates the elaborate ladders and six electric lights which were developed by Bulleid (the original design on No 21C1 had only grab rails and footsteps, no ladders). Also visible are the bearing springs with link hangers, a feature of the first 10 tenders. The blue livery was abandoned in May 1951, and the first 'Merchant Navy' to appear in the standard dark green was No 35024.   *C. G. Geard*

Above:
Comparison with the official works photo of this engine taken when just built at Eastleigh in September 1941 (see page 22), clearly shows the quite substantial alterations made to the front end layout; in an effort to improve smoke deflection and draughting. The locomotive is still in the postwar SR Malachite green livery but has received its new BR number, and the tender is lettered with the new owner's name in full, pending the design and introduction of the lion and wheel totem. No 35003 *Royal Mail* is seen at the head of the 'Atlantic Coast Express', standing at Exeter Central *circa* 1948/9. *Ian Allan Library*

With a tractive effort of 37 500lb at 85per cent of boiler pressure the new Pacifics were certainly powerful machines and despite a number of persistent teething troubles they could run freely, although restricted to the Salisbury – Exeter line (1942-44). Another 10 were ordered, which had a number of differences, and which weighed more, at 94¾tons in full working order. In particular the boiler was altered. Whereas the first 10 boilers, built at Glasgow, had the front ring of the barrel tapered on the underside and the rear ring parallel, the last 20 boilers built (at Eastleigh) together with five spare boilers, had the front ring parallel and the rear ring tapered along the bottom, which had the effect of reducing weight and water capacity, but not the heating surface. The layout of the sanding gear was altered (see page 95) and there were improvements to the design of the cab and tender. Other detail alterations are shown in the accompanying illustrations.

A third, and final, batch of 10 'Merchant Navy' Pacifics emerged in the early days of nationalisation, and never carried the odd Bulleid numbering system – becoming instead BR Nos 35021-30. These had further detail alterations, including modified cabs and longer smoke deflectors and were fitted from new with TIA water treatment apparatus. These were given 6000gal tenders (in most cases they at

Above:
In the 1950s a close study was still being made of the performance of modern steam locomotives and one aid to this was the self-weighing tender, which allowed an accurate record to be kept of fuel consumption in everyday service, as well as trial running or testing. Locomotives on each Region were selected to run with self-weighing tenders, and the Southern fitted a 6,000gal version to No 35018 in 1952. The tender carried TIA (Traîtement Intégrale Armand) water treatment equipment, with the tank visible on the rear end of the tender, alongside the vacuum reservoirs. The TIA scheme was applied to the last 10 engines, Nos 35021-30, when new, and gradually extended to the rest of the class. *L. Elsey*

Left:
No 35019 *French Line C.G.T.* was fitted with a single blastpipe and normal diameter chimney, in 1951, under the auspices of R. G. Jarvis. The engine is seen arriving at Salisbury one hot noonday in July 1953. From this angle, the tunnel between the tender sides and the coal space is clearly visible. Another modification introduced by Jarvis, after Bulleid had left the Southern, was the lowering of the boiler pressure from 280 to 250lb psi. All but eight of the class were so treated before the rebuilding programme commenced in 1956. The single chimney was not adopted, however, and No 35019 reverted to the multiple-jet arrangement for the remainder of her career, including the final rebuilt form. Another experiment was undertaken at this time, when No 35014 was fitted with a boiler without thermic syphons. *G. F. Heiron*

first had borrowed 4,500/5,500 gal tenders). The forward water filling points were not fitted. On this last batch of engines the trailing truck frame was of fabricated steel plate, instead of the one-piece steel casting previously used, in order to reduce weight.

The engines were built as follows:

Nos 21C1-21C10	Eastleigh	1941/2
Nos 21C11-21C20	Eastleigh	1944/5
Nos 35021-35030	Eastleigh	1948/9

Nos 21C1-21C20 were renumbered 35001-35020 by British Railways, in 1948.

Despite many modifications after No 21C1 appeared in 1941, it was apparent to the men on the ground that many of the features which were intended to ease their job did precisely the opposite. The oil bath, the valve motion, the steam reverser and the difficulties of access created by the air-smoothed casing, all contributed to costly and excessive maintenance when compared to more conventional steam designs of equivalent size and power. An early step taken by BR was the reduction of the boiler pressure from 280 to 250lb psi which had the effect of reducing their tendency to chronic bouts of slipping. In any case, the footplatemen tended to run the engines quite happily at less than the 280lb.

Inevitably, the case for modification won the day, thereby bringing the engines more into line with contemporary BR standard practice, by removing the more unorthodox features. The subsequent history of the 'Merchant Navy' Pacifics in their modified form is described in, Section 6, on pages 78 - 89, including dates of rebuilding and withdrawal.

Above:
By 1955 the self-weighing tender had been attached to No 35014 *Nederland Line*, seen here at Eastleigh on 9 April 1955, after attention at the works. The livery scheme has lost the original simplicity, with the cab sides lined to match the tender rather than the sides of the boiler. The casing ahead of the cylinders has been removed, giving a more angular appearance to the front end, and the forward sanding gear has been removed together with the protective cover over the slidebars. *F. Gambin*

Top right:
In November 1956, No 35010 *Blue Star*, was stored at Bournemouth Central awaiting removal to Eastleigh for rebuilding. This was the first of the initial 10 members of the class to be selected for rebuilding; all previous examples had been from the later 20 engines. During rebuilding of No 35010 it proved necessary to renew the main frames ahead of the cylinders. As seen here the locomotive illustrates the final condition of the early Bulleid Pacifics, with revised cab design, smoke deflectors and trough, and air-smoothed casing removed ahead of the cylinders. The tender is still in basically original state. No 35010 emerged from Eastleigh in rebuilt form in January 1957, and by October 1959 all 30 engines were dealt with, the last two being Nos 35006/28. This view of No 35010 clearly illustrates the curved cutaway of the air-smoothed casing, above the driving wheels; a feature of the first 10 engines, also the horizontal rib midway down the casing (introduced on Nos 21C3-10). *C. P. Boocock*

Centre right:
Additional train nameboards were attached to the smoke deflectors for the locomotive working the 'Devon Belle' Pullman, finished in red and yellow. With a light load of five cars, plus the observation car at the rear, 'Merchant Navy' No 35021 *New Zealand Line* is seen at Winchfield on 13 July 1957. The engine is attached to a rebuilt tender, although not itself converted until two years later. In fact modification of the tenders was commenced in 1952, with removal of the raves to allow easier access for water filling. *M. W. Earley*

Left:
One of the last 'Merchant Navy' Pacifics to be rebuilt was the pioneer No 35001 *Channel Packet* and in the interim period it was attached to a rebuilt tender for service on the Eastern Section, to which it returned in 1957. The engine is seen working a down Belgian Boat Express near Ashford in the August of that year, with a Class L 4-4-0 on the adjacent track. Comparison with the picture of No 35001 (as 21C1) on page 19, clearly shows the extent of the modifications since 1946, in particular to the front end and the cab. *Channel Packet* was rebuilt at Eastleigh in August 1959. The subsequent careers of the rebuilt 'Merchant Navy' Pacifics forms the content of Section 6, on pages 78-89. *P. Ransome-Wallis*

0–6–0 Class Q1 (BR power class 5F) Goods Engines

Introduced: 1942
Total: 40
'Austerity'

The final locomotive design produced by R. E. L. Maunsell before his retirement was a modest 0–6–0 derived mainly from existing standard parts, and intended for use on certain lines where weight restrictions had meant the prolonged retention of pre-Grouping types, such as the LSWR Adams and SER Stirling goods engines. This new Maunsell class Q was in the pipeline when Bulleid arrived on the Southern, and he is reported to have regretted the fact that he arrived too late to have building halted. He categorised them as pedestrian and nondescript for a design produced as late as 1938.

Circumstances were to change drastically in a short space of time, with the outbreak of World War 2, and O. V. S. Bulleid was presented with a traffic requirement for an 0–6–0 locomotive to be capable of operating the heavier loads of wartime over the same secondary routes as the Maunsell Q, which had a total weight of less than 54tons for the engine. As Bulleid himself explained at a talk to Feltham enginemen in November 1942, the easiest course would have been to build a further 40 Qs, but experience with the existing engines had shown that the motion and cylinder design left something to be desired, and the boiler capacity was somewhat less than

Right:
Photographed just before the final coat of black paint was applied, newly completed 0-6-0 No C1 outside Brighton Works. An interesting deviation from the finalised livery is evident in the very high position of the lettering on the tender. At this stage the numerals and lettering were on metal plates attached to the engine. The lack of running-plate emphasised the BFB wheels, which were about 10% lighter than the conventional spoked type. The locomotive frame was lightened wherever possible, and fabricated details were used instead of steel castings. Essentially an austerity design, Bulleid intended it to have a relatively short life, with a minimum of overhaul. In fact, the class was destined to operate for some 26 years!
British Rail

Below right:
Nothing quite like No C1 had been delivered from a British locomotive works before, and the emergence of Bulleid's new concept of the classic 0-6-0 maid-of-all-work, in the midst of war, provoked an immediate outcry from enthusiasts who were shocked by the apparent disregard for aesthetic appearance. The first of the class is seen here in as-built condition, at Brighton on 26 March 1942 in plain black livery with yellow lettering shaded in green. The tender, which was largely of welded construction, was similar to the 'Merchant Navy' Pacific's design, but had the bearing springs attached to brackets (later also applied to the Pacific version). The tender cab was linked by rubber bellows, at roof level, to the engine cab. Both live-steam injectors were mounted on the fireman's side. Tender capacity was 3,700gal and 5ton of coal, with the coal space designed to be self-trimming.
British Rail

Below:
'Q1' class 0-6-0, as built.

Far left:
Unlike the Pacifics, the new 0-6-0s were not fitted with electric lighting and there was a noticeable lack of handrails at the front end. A curious and unnecessary ornamentation of No C1 was the small plate at first attached to the bufferbeam, which displayed the locomotive number on a black background. Provision of a steam heating hose was largely to allow their use on empty coaching stock workings. *British Rail SR*

Left:
Tender end detail of 0-6-0 No C1, taken at Brighton on 27 February 1942, showing very well the clean and simple layout and welded construction. Vacuum cylinders are located below bufferbeam, to the rear of the rear axle. *British Rail SR*

Below:
Class Q1 0-6-0 No C21 is seen heading a down goods near Winchester in 1948. The lettering 'Southern' on the tender is now centrally placed and grab rails have been added to the smokebox door, and surround. The locomotive number is painted directly on to the bufferbeam. A sliding shutter has been added to the cutaway at the leading end of the tender, which gave access to the tank fillers. *Donovan E. H. Box*

the new traffic demands required; he therefore set his sights higher.

In peacetime conditions the Southern was primarily a passenger-carrying line and therefore possessed a large number of passenger and mixed-traffic locomotives which, although allowed over many of the secondary routes which were suddenly the focus of wartime goods traffic, were deficient in power for wartime needs. Thus was born the idea of Bulleid's second locomotive for the Southern Railway, an Austerity 0–6–0 with the largest boiler that could be accommodated on the chassis, and with the weight kept to the minimum by frugal design. The Q1 class had a high tractive effort, of 30 000lb (compared to the 26 157lb of the Maunsell Q class engines) and yet could operate over all but 7per cent of SR routes.

To achieve this remarkable version of the classic British 0–6–0 maid-of-all-work, Bulleid went back to basic principles in design, doing away with all unnecessary ornamentation and dispensing with a number of customary features. Because of the war it was not possible to obtain generous allocations of steel for

locomotive construction, so in order to keep the weight down to the required figure he departed from convention in locomotive appearance and produced a 'bare' apparition which had the more conservative students of British steam locomotive design in an uproar.

The firebox was based on that of the Maunsell 'Lord Nelson' class and the same press blocks were used for the throat-plate and back-plate as for that class, which was in itself a useful economy. The grate area of 27sq ft was the largest of any British 0–6–0. The boiler barrel was in one piece, tapered equally on top and bottom from 5ft 9in to 5ft outside – dimensions which were the largest size consistent with providing the driver with a good lookout that came within the loading gauge requirement. The length of the barrel, 9ft $9\frac{1}{4}$in, was dictated by the length of the firebox. The total heating surface was 1860sq ft, with the firebox providing 170sq ft, the tubes and flues 1472-sq ft and the superheater 218sq ft. The boiler pressure at 230lb was high for an 0–6–0 and tractive effort was, as stated earlier, 30 000lb at 85per cent boiler pressure.

The revolutionary exterior finish was partly

governed by the need to reduce weight, as already explained, but also partly to simplify manufacture. The boiler lagging was a product known as Idaglass, and in order that this should not bear any weight the boiler casing was carried directly on the frames, instead of embracing the barrel. Two brackets supported the casing, which was in two sections. The traditional running boards above the wheels were dispensed with, saving 17cwt, and the boiler casing was squared-off at the lower edge to create rudimentary splashers for the coupled wheels. The smokebox was shaped so as to provide a greater volume than the largest circular one which could have been fitted, also leaving more room for maintenance and repair procedures. The upper shape of the smokebox was echoed in the shape of the two sections of boiler casing, producing a distinctive contour. The five-nozzle multiple-jet blastpipe was provided with a basic stovepipe chimney and the dome cover was similarly lacking in ornamentation.

The two inside cylinders, of 19in diameter by 26in stroke, had overhead piston valves with outside admission operated by Stephenson link

Far left:
Renumbered No 33018 by BR, Class Q1 0-6-0 (formerly No C18) trundles through Raynes Park on a down local freight on 25 June 1965. The shield behind the screw coupling, attached to the bufferbeam by two brackets, was to protect the BR/AWS equipment; latterly carried by some of the class. *M. S. Stokes*

Above left:
Comparison with the photo of No C1 when new, on page 38, shows the grab rails which were added to the smokebox door and surround and the slightly revised lampbrackets on the smokebox door, and BR cast iron numberplate added; No 33019 otherwise betrays little change since built.
D. Sutton Collection/Ian Allan Library

Above:
Hauling ballast for sea wall repairs, 'Q1' 0-6-0 No 33007 makes a fine sight as she climbs the 1 in 100 up from Herne Bay. When new, the pioneer engine No C1 worked a trial trip over the 24 miles from Woking to Basingstoke with a mixed train of approximately 1,000 ton, taking 58min without extending the locomotive. The booked time for 800ton was then 66min.
P. Ransome-Wallis

motion, giving a maximum travel of $6\frac{7}{8}$in; the reversing gear was steam-operated. The cast steel box wheels were of the same Bulleid-Firth-Brown patent type as introduced with the 'Merchant Navy' Pacifics, and had a diameter of 5ft 1in. The wheelbase was the same as for the Q class (see diagram) and the cylinders were in the same position.

To quote Bulleid's own words: 'The result was an engine having a light weight of only 45tons 18cwt. By fabricating and the use of thin plates, the weight of the tender was reduced to 16tons. An engine and tender of normal design would be about 14tons heavier, so on 40 engines 560tons of weight has been saved. This is equal to about 700tons of raw materials, equal to nine more engines and tenders. And the completed engine complied with the Engineer's limitations'.

The engines were built as follows:

Nos C1–C16	Brighton	1942
Nos C17–C36	Ashford	1942
Nos C37–C40	Brighton	1942

The 1946 locomotive building programme for the Southern Railway included a further 20 0–6–0 locomotives. These did not come to fruition, but some material was ordered for parts, and the early schemes for the 'Leader' class (see page 66) were intended to make use of these parts, although the final design did not in fact incorporate them. In his post-war plan for standard locomotives Bulleid did not include the Q1 0–6–0s, partly because of their somewhat restricted brake power on unfitted

Above:
Cross-London transfer freights were one of the duties performed by the 'Q1' 0-6-0s, and during World War 2 they hauled some remarkable loads for their size. In BR days No 33013 was photographed passing Graham Road signalbox with a westbound transfer freight on 21 March 1959. In the background an Eastern Region Class N7 0-6-0T can be seen passing overhead with a Liverpool Street-Enfield Town train, approaching Hackney Downs station. *K. L. Cook*

Above right:
An 11-coach train of Western Region stock forms the Hastings-Birmingham relief train, seen passing Cooksbridge in the charge of No33036 on 6 August, 1960. The 'Q1s' proved themselves capable of a fair turn of speed on such passenger duties, up to 75mph, although the enginemen were not enamoured of the spectacle of the side rods (clearly visible from the cab) in motion at such times, due to the lack of footplate or splashers, and rain water was thrown up, restricting forward vision by forcing the driver to take cover! *S. C. Nash*

freights. Nevertheless, the 40 engines built proved themselves most worthy members of the motive power stud, and perhaps over the years one even became accustomed to their unorthodox appearance!

First of Class Withdrawn: 33028 (1963)
Last of Class Withdrawn: 33006/20/7 (1966)

Above:
Another view of No 33013, in final condition, with additional mud-hole washout plugs on the firebox side. The large sandboxes between the coupled wheels are well illustrated together with the leading sandbox, which was integral with the footstep and bufferbeam. The overall appearance of the 'Q1's remained the same throughout their careers. To No 33028 of the class fell the doubtful honour of being the first Bulleid engine (apart from the ill-fated 'Leader' class and the CIE 'Turf Burner') to be withdrawn from service, February 1963, due to a defective cylinder. This marked the commencement of the onslaught which was to see Bulleid steam vanish in such a dramatic manner over the next four years.
J. C. Haydon

SECTION 3(a)

4–6–2 Class WC (BR power class 7P*)
Passenger Engines

Introduced: 1945
Total: 66†
'West Country'

* *Originally 6P; later 7P5F.*
† *Total for 'West Country' class out of grand total of 110 Light Pacific's*

Apparently undaunted by the prolonged teething troubles experienced with his first Pacific design, Bulleid pressed ahead with the design of a lightweight scaled-down version; intended for use on the many restricted secondary routes (apart from a few branch lines) which the SR owned, and over which the 'Merchant Navy' class were prohibited on account of weight.

In June 1945, just as Britain was celebrating the long hoped-for cessation of the war in Europe, and beginning to look to the future, the first Light Pacific was completed at Brighton Works and very appropriately turned out in full Malachite green livery, instead of the dead black of wartime. As the priority area for service was the West Country and the West of England main line, the Southern decided to call the new Pacifics the 'West Country' class. They were intended for both passenger and freight trains (the latter essentially vacuum-fitted) and they were generally similar in appearance to the 'Merchant Navy' class. Comparison with the

larger Pacifics showed that the chief dimensional differences were the cylinder bore, reduced by $1\frac{5}{8}$in to $16\frac{3}{8}$in; the piston stroke was the same, at 24in; the grate area was reduced to 38.25sq ft from $48\frac{1}{2}$sq ft; and the evaporative and superheating surfaces were

Top right:
First of the class, No 21C101 *Exeter* in as-built condition, with full postwar livery of Malachite green but with *painted* name and shield. In effect the 'West Country' was a scaled-down, lightweight version of the 'Merchant Navy', with a reduced axle-load and restricted loading guage, intended for use on the many secondary routes where the larger Pacifics were not allowed. The cab width was reduced to 8ft 6in (compared with 9ft for a 'Merchant Navy') and the locomotive weight was brought down to 86 tons, with a tender weighing $42\frac{1}{2}$ tons and carrying 5ton of coal and 4,500gal of water. The overall appearance closely followed that of the larger Pacifics, although for some reason difficult to define, they seemed the neater of the two Pacific designs. No 21C101 was officially named at Exeter station on 10 July 1945.
Author's Collection

Below right:
An imposing study of 'West Country' Pacific No 21C126 in original condition; taken at Victoria in 1947. The nameplates *Yes Tor* were not yet fitted. A criticism of these engines, with their narrower cab and smoke deflectors, was their restricted forward visibility for the enginemen. The very short smoke deflectors were later lengthened somewhat, and the cab front windows improved.   *C. R. L. Coles*

Below:
The diagram illustrates the initial batch of 'West Country' Pacifics, as built.

respectively 329 and 277sq ft less, at 2122 sq ft and 545sq ft. Boiler pressure was the same, at 280lb psi. The boiler barrel length was reduced by only $1\frac{1}{2}$in, but the diameter at the front was reduced to 5ft 6in, compared to 5ft $9\frac{3}{4}$in.

The shorter firebox allowed a reduction of 1ft for the distance between the trailing truck and the rear coupled axle (9ft) and the overall wheelbase was reduced to 35ft 6in, compared to 36ft 9in for a 'Merchant Navy'. The locomotive weight was effectively reduced from $94\frac{3}{4}$tons to 86tons. The weight on each coupled axle was 18tons 15cwt (against the 21tons of the 'Merchant Navy'), the bogie carried 15tons 10cwt and the trailing axle was loaded to 14tons 5cwt. The tender fitted had a water capacity of 4500gal and 5tons of coal, and weighed $42\frac{1}{2}$tons in working order, compared to $47\frac{3}{4}$tons for the larger tenders. The tractive effort, at 85per cent of working pressure, was 31 000lb against the 37 500lb of the larger engine. In fact, the Maunsell 'Lord Nelson' was theoretically more powerful, with a tractive effort of 33 510lb, but with their larger boilers the Light Pacifics proved themselves superior in sustained haulage capacity and turn of speed, although heavier on coal.

No less than 70 of the new class were ordered in one go and there seems to have been

Above:
No 21C138, as yet un-named (later *Lynton*), is seen passing Sydenham Hill with an up morning Continental boat train for Victoria. The very narrow forward cab window is evident in this view; a distinct improvement was later made, with the introduction of the wedge shape (see next illustration), and in the final 40 engines the cab was 9ft wide instead of 8ft 6in. In August 1946 the Government announced a plan for the conversion of over 1,000 steam locomotives of all four railways, to burn oil instead of coal. The Southern included 20 'West Country' Pacifics in their list of chosen engines. First of the class to be converted was No 21C119 *Bideford*, in July 1947, followed by No 21C136 *Westward Ho!*, which had more sophisticated and successful equipment. The Government then proceeded to abandon the project, and both engines were soon restored to coal burning.   *E. R. Wethersett*

none of the hesitation which surrounded the larger Pacifics in their early days. The 'West Country' class soon made an impression on services west of Exeter, at last relieving the hard-working 2–6–0s of Maunsell's U and N classes which had soldiered on with the heavier loads of wartime. In order to allow the new engines the widest possible route availability Bulleid restricted the cab width to 8ft 6in, compared to 9ft, so that they could be used on the Tonbridge and Hastings route, although this never materialised.

Most of the features that Bulleid had introduced with the 'Merchant Navy' class were perpetuated in the lightweight engines, including the air-smoothed casing, the patent valve gear, the BFB wheel centres, the clasp brakes, the thermic syphons and the oil bath enclosing the motion. Welding was again widely used in the construction of the engine and tender, and was an important factor in weight saving. Like the 'Merchant Navy' class, the Light Pacifics were fitted with turbo-generators providing current for the headcode lamps on engine and tender, the cab and gauge lamps and the illumination of details for examination purposes.

As mentioned above, the new engines were never used over the restricted Tonbridge-Hastings route, so the reduced width of the cab was not necessary. Some criticism was forthcoming on the limited forward visibility which resulted, and various experiments with smoke deflector design took place, as can be seen in the accompanying illustrations. Finally, the flat-fronted cab was altered to a wedge shape which enabled a larger window to be fitted. Commencing with Battle of Britain class No 21C164 (see page 56) this modification was applied as the engine were built, and from No 34071 onwards the cab width was increased to 9ft.

Confusion sometimes arises from the Southern Railway's decision to label the

Above:
Immediately apparent is the extension of the smoke deflector wingplates to roughly twice their original length, on No 34006 *Bude* seen here outside Marylebone Station during the 1948 Locomotive Exchange Trials attached to the ER Dynamometer Car. The engine is attached to an LMS Stanier water-scoop tender (painted black) for use during the trials. Nos 34004/5/6 were selected to represent the class in the Exchanges, all with LMS tenders. The engines put up some really sparkling performances, particularly in Scotland, where No 34004 worked on the Perth-Inverness section, fitted with tablet apparatus. The cab has been rebuilt with a wedge shape at the front, to improve forward visibility. Only Nos 34004/5/6, the 1948 exchange trial engines, carried these extra-long smoke deflectors. *E. R. Wethersett*

Below:
No 34011 *Tavistock* was one of the SR locomotives selected for experimental liveries in 1948, by the newly created Railway Executive, and the travelling public were asked to state their opinions. In a very bright apple green with red, yellow and grey lining, No 34011 also wears the red and yellow 'Devon Belle' headboards. Photographed at Exmouth Junction, 28 July 1949. *N. E. Preedy*

Bottom:
A compromise lengthening of the smoke deflectors is seen here on No 34048 *Crediton*, which also has the revised cab window design. Malachite green livery, with BR Gill Sans numerals and no totem or lettering on the tender. Photographed at Exeter Central.
Ian Allan Library

Right:
No 34039 *Boscastle*, in Malachite green but with new BR numbering and lettering, shows a further variation of smoke deflector design – extended forward almost to become vertical alongside the smokebox.
Ian Allan Library

Below right:
Commencing with No 34091 a further series of 'West Country' Pacifics appeared, up to No 34108. These never carried Malachite green livery, appearing instead in the standard dark BR Brunswick green, with orange and black lining and lion and wheel emblem, as seen here on No 34103 *Calstock,* working the 'Golden Arrow' Pullman in fine style through the chalk cuttings of the North Kent downs. These had tenders of 5,500gal capacity, weighing 47.25tons. These engines had a 9ft-wide cab, and wedge-shape front cab windows from new. *F. R. Hebron*

engines as two different classes, as they were in actuality all the same. However, the publicity which this created was certainly worthwhile and I have followed their example by describing the 'Battle of Britain' engines in a separate subsection, on pages 56-65. The first of the 'Battle of Britain' series was No 21C149, although it ran for some time without nameplates and was at first described as a 'West Country' – just to add to the confusion.

Some truly brilliant performances, by keen enginemen made the Light Pacific design one of the stars of the 1948 Locomotive Exchanges (in which three 'West Country' engines participated, Nos 34004/5/6, ex-Nos 21C104/5/6) although the published results of the tests later revealed a heavy coal consumption. The lightweight Pacifics were to display all the

Top:
Although in BR Brunswick green livery and with the front-end casing removed ahead of the cylinders, No 34028 *Eddystone* still carried the original cab when this photograph was taken. No 34028 was selected for rebuilding by BR and of course received a wider 9ft cab with wedge-shape windows in the process; it reappeared in the rebuilt state in March 1958, (see section 7, page 90, for details of the rebuilt Light Pacifics). *J. Davenport*

Above:
Before the BR rebuilding scheme commenced, there was always a degree of fascination in viewing a Bulleid Pacific in the partially undressed state which workshop overhaul produced. It was a reminder of the orthodox appearance of the 'works' beneath the air-smoothed shroud, and an indication of the inconvenience caused to maintenance staff. A bogie with BFB wheels is in the foreground; the locomotive is No 34038 *Lynton*, photographed in July 1953. *R. H. Clark*

same weaknesses as their larger brethren as time went on, and eventually they were selected for rebuilding along very similar lines, as described in Section 7 on pages 90–97. But it would be less than justice to dismiss these remarkable engines in such a manner. If they had their failings, they also had many fine qualities, including a wonderful boiler of incredible steaming capacity. Their reduced weight allowed them to roam far and wide over the Southern system, and they were the first engines larger than the N class 2–6–0s, allowed to travel over the Meldon Viaduct. During the Locomotive Exchanges they broke new ground for the Pacific wheel arrangement over the Highland line from Perth to Inverness and the Midland line from St Pancras to Manchester.

Construction of the Bulleid Light Pacifics was to continue after he had retired from the nationalised Southern Region in September 1949, and a total of 110 locomotives of the 'West Country' and 'Battle of Britain' classes was completed when 'Battle of Britain' No. 34110 66 Squadron appeared from Brighton in January 1951. Some speculation had surrounded this final engine of the class, which was delayed in construction for some months (No 34109 had been completed in May 1950) and rumour had it that the engine would not have Bulleid's valve gear. Nonetheless, it emerged in due course in full Bulleid form, in the very same month that the first BR standard two-cylinder Pacific No. 70000 Britannia appeared from Crewe. The tide was turning against the Bulleid engines and some of them had very short careers before rebuilding, as described in Section 7, after which they had a

Above:
Comparison with the picture of No 34028 opposite shows some further modifications that were made to the 'West Country' locomotives in BR days. The cab has the improved wedge-shape front windows, and the tender has been cut down. The air-smoothed casing ahead of the cylinders has been removed and the locomotive carries BR AWS equipment on the front end. This was one of the 50 Light Pacifics which were never rebuilt by BR, and is seen here in the final form in which it ran. No 34041 Wilton was photographed in ex-works condition at Eastleigh on 10 October 1963. The livery of locomotive and tender no longer matched, and the smooth lines of Bulleid's original conception were completely disrupted by the various modifications that had been made.
G. Wheeler

family resemblance to the standard BR Pacifics. So late in the day was this programme of rebuilding undertaken that financial justification did not exist for the rebuilding of all 110 locomotives, and 50 were left to run out their days in original Bulleid form. No 34104 was the last to be rebuilt, in May 1961.

The 'West Country' class engines were built as follows:

Nos 21C101-21C148	Brighton	1945/6
Nos 34091-34108	Brighton	1949/50
	Eastleigh*	

Nos 21C101-21C148 were renumbered 34001-34048 respectively in 1948, by British Railways.

*Nos 34095/7/9/101/2/4 built at Eastleigh

Below:
A very characteristic study of a Light Pacific on the move, with copious exhaust! No 34033 *Honiton* was photographed near Mannamend on Sunday 15 July 1956, working 'wrong line' during engineering works, (note the red warning flag perched on the nearest track) and was heading a Plymouth-Waterloo express in fine style. *R. C. Riley*

Left:
A number of attempts were made to improve the draughting and exhaust dispersal of the Light Pacifics over a period of years; one such attempt is seen here, on No 34035 *Shaftesbury*, which had the cowling carried down to join the smoke deflectors (similar to the wartime experiments on No 21C10, see page 24). The engine is seen in this modified form, at Eastleigh on 12 April 1960, with BR AWS equipment on the front end. Another experiment was made on 'Battle of Britain' No 34049, as illustrated on page 62. *L. Elsey*

Below:
Coaling operations at Bournemouth motive power depot, with the aid of a mechanical shovel, 7 June 1965. The rebuilt tender of No 34103 *Calstock* is well illustrated, with the electric lighting and two welded tubular ladders on the rear. Although 25kV catenary electrification warning signs are also carried, the engines seldom found themselves in such a location. *P. L. Simpson*

Modifications were made to the tender by BR, by removing the raves to allow the water column bag to swing across the back, without obstruction, when filling the tank: No 34043 was the first to receive a modified tender, in June 1952. In common with the 'Merchant Navy' Pacifics the boiler pressure of all the Light Pacifics was reduced from 280lb to 250lb psi over a period of some two years from 1954-6. Rebuilding commenced in the summer of 1957 with No 34005 *Barnstaple*.

†*First of West Country Class Withdrawn (Unrebuilt):* 34035, 34043 (1963)
Last of West Country Class Withdrawn (Unrebuilt): 34023, 34102 (1967)
†*Withdrawal dates for the rebuilt engines are given on page 97.*

SECTION 3(b)

4–6–2 Class BB (BR power class 7P*) Passenger Engines
Introduced: 1946
Total: 44†
'Battle of Britain'

*Originally 6P, later given as 7P5F.

†Total for Battle of Britain class, out of grand total of 110 Light Pacifics

The decision to name some of the Light Pacifics in honour of the Battle of Britain was an excellent piece of public relations work, coming so soon after the restoration of peacetime working on the Southern Railway, and it undoubtedly helped to bring Bulleid's engines to the attention of the public at large. They were identical to the 'West Country' class, but tended to be thought of as a separate entity, and I have therefore segregated them accordingly.

The first naming ceremonies were suitably near the anniversary date of the Battle of Britain, in September 1947, by which time a number had run for some months without nameplates, and a particularly nice gesture was the choice of name for No. 34090 (last of a batch of 20 built in 1948/9,) which became *Sir Eustace Missenden Southern Railway*, and received full SR Malachite green livery.

It was a member of the 'Battle of Britain' class which was involved in the Lewisham disaster of 4 December 1957, at the Nunhead Flyover between Lewisham St. John's and Park Bridge. The locomotive, No 34066 *Spitfire*, was working the 4.56pm down Cannon Street to Ramsgate train when it collided in foggy weather with the rear of the 5.18pm electric train from Charing Cross to Hayes. The crash also involved a train passing over the flyover

Right:
Freak numbering for *Biggin Hill* in the early months of nationalisation; the Bulleid notation has had the prefix 'S' (denoting Southern Region) added, to become S21C157, whilst the smokebox carries neither the Bulleid circular brass SR ownership plate, nor the later BR standard smokebox numberplate. The casing ahead of the right-hand cylinder appears to have taken a knock; this portion of casing was later removed from the class. *E. R. Wethersett*

Below right:
Modified smoke deflectors were fitted to No 21C162 (later No 34062 *17 Squadron*), when built at Brighton in 1947; without any great improvement upon smoke dispersal, however.
Crown Copyright. National Railway Museum

Below:
'Battle of Britain' Pacific No 21C164 (later named *Fighter Command*) had the honour of being the 1,000th locomotive built at Brighton Works. A special ceremony was held in the works yard on June 1947 to commemorate the event. Coupled to the Pacific was the ex-LBSCR Stroudley 'Terrier' 0-6-0T No 82 *Boxhill*, which was restored to the famous Stroudley livery of 'improved engine green'. The two locomotives provided a truly remarkable contrast in aesthetic form. The Bulleid engine is seen here with the original cab design, but it actually entered traffic with the modified cab, being the first locomotive to receive this.
P. F. Winding

and 90 people died in the ghastly pile-up. The engine was repaired and later returned to traffic.

The 'Battle of Britain' class engines were built as follows:

Nos 21C149-21C170	Brighton	1946/7
Nos 34071-34090	Brighton	1948/9
Nos 34109-34110	Brighton	1950/1

Nos 21C149-21C170 were renumbered 34049-34070 respectively, by BR in 1948.

No doubt because they were newer than the 'West Country' engines (except for Nos. 34091-34108) the 'Battle of Britain' engines were less affected by the BR rebuilding programme. Only 17 engines out of a total of 44 were rebuilt, compared with 43 'West Country' class out of a total of 66.

†*First of 'Battle of Britain' Class Withdrawn (Unrebuilt):* 34055 (1963).

Last of 'Battle of Britain' Class Withdrawn (Unrebuilt): 34057 (1967)
†*Withdrawal dates for the rebuilt engines are given on page 97.*

Right:
Experimental livery of apple green with red, cream and grey lining and Gill sans lettering and numerals, applied to No 34086 (later named *219 Squadron*) at Brighton works, as part of an attempt to decide the new locomotive liveries for the nationalised system in 1948 (see also page 50). The thin lining was not as effective as Bulleid's original scheme. *Lens of Sutton*

Below:
Brand-new Pacific No 34076 (later named *41 Squadron*) in Bulleid livery but carrying BR numbering and lettering, painted in Southern style. From No 34071 onwards the Bulleid notation was never applied, as the locomotives were delivered after nationalisation. These engines were built new with the wider 9ft cab and had sweptback, wedge-shaped cab-front windows, which were later applied to the earlier batch on rebuilding (see pages 91-92). *Ian Allan Library*

Above:
Although not constructed until February 1949, 'Battle of Britain' Pacific No 34090 was finished in full Southern Railway livery of Malachite green, with yellow lining and black trim; however, the new BR emblem appeared on the tender. The reason behind this was the choice of name for the locomotive – *Sir Eustace Missenden, Southern Railway* – a tribute to the last General Manager of the system prior to nationalisation. Illustrated is the tender of No 34090 in as-built condition. Tender capacity of Nos 34071-90 was 5,500 gal. *British Rail SR.*

Left:
Stewarts Lane could always be relied upon to turn out an immaculate locomotive for a special such as a royal train, or the visit of a foreign dignity. Witness the beautiful grooming of the front end of 'Battle of Britain' Pacific No 34088 *213 Squadron* when selected to work the royal train conveying the Emperor of Ethiopia on the occasion of his state visit, 14-16 October 1954. *British Rail SR*

Above:
In May 1949, 'Battle of Britain' Pacific No 34059 *Sir Archibald Sinclair* was loaned to the Great Eastern section of the Eastern Region, where it worked to Norwich and Parkeston Quay. In 1951 three Light Pacifics were on loan to Stratford shed, and two ER 'Britannia' Pacifics (Nos 70009/14) were on loan to the Southern, later followed by No 70004 which was exhibited at the Festival of Britain. The Bulleid engines were not popular with the GE crews and soon returned home. No 34057 *Biggin Hill* is seen here approaching Seven Kings with a Sunday excursion out of Liverpool Street, on 3 June 1951. *K. E. Huckle*

Top left:
'Battle of Britain' class 4-6-2 No 34055 *Fighter Pilot*, photographed at Salisbury shed on 6 June 1959 in BR Brunswick green livery. The portion of casing ahead of the cylinders has been removed, but otherwise the engine is substantially in original condition, except for the modified cab windows. *P. H. Wells*

Centre left:
The problems of smoke deflection and draughting remained unresolved until the BR rebuilding removed the air-smoothed casing entirely, greatly improving those members of the WC and BB lightweights which were so dealt with. Many experiments were tried on the Bulleid Pacifics, including complete removal of the smoke deflector wingplates, as seen here, on No 34049 *Anti-Aircraft Command,* photographed at Eastleigh on 19 February 1960. Note the handholds cut into the front end of the air-smoothed casing, and the continuation of the side sheets into the cowling ahead of the chimney. *L. Elsey*

Bottom left:
The tenders of most Light Pacifics were rebuilt in cut-down form, irrespective of whether the locomotive was selected for rebuilding or not. No 34051 *Winston Churchill* is seen here in ex-works condition at Eastleigh on 13 October 1963, carrying BR AWS equipment and 25kV warning signs on the front end. On 30 January 1965 this locomotive had the sad distinction of hauling the special funeral train conveying the body of Sir Winston Churchill, from Waterloo to Handborough. *G. Wheeler*

Below:
Time took its toll on the air-smoothed outer casing of Bulleid's Pacifics, as is clearly seen in the raking light falling on No 34057 *Biggin Hill,* photographed in the shed yard at Nine Elms one February night.
V. C. K. Allen

Above:
Close-up of the characteristic narrow chimney of the Giesl Oblong Ejector, fitted to No 34064 in August 1962. Seven nozzles, with blower jets between them, were arranged in line to exhaust upwards to the narrow chimney, with a notable improvement in the draughting. A scheme to fit 20 or so more of the unmodified Light Pacifics was not pursued, as by this time expenditure on steam was not regarded with favour by BR management, although the performance of No 34064 after this modification was generally excellent. The main reason for the experiment was an attempt to reduce the sparkthrowing characteristic of the Bulleid engines, an unfortunate feature which was not appreciated by farmers and other lineside dwellers. *P. H. Groom*

Left:
Nearing Padstow with the 'Atlantic Coast Express' from Waterloo on 8 May 1964, 'Battle of Britain' No 34054 *Lord Beaverbrook* makes a pleasing picture and provides a useful comparison to the illustration above showing the wide diameter chimney of the Bulleid multiple-jet blastpipe. *S. C. Nash*

0–6–6–0T 'Leader' class
(BR power class 5MT)
Mixed-Traffic Engines
Introduced: 1949
Total: 1*

*Five were ordered and three were brought to an advanced stage of construction but only one entered trial service.

It was in the course of his presidential address to the Institute of Mechanical Engineers, in October 1946, that Bulleid first revealed to the public his new concept in tank engine design, stating that the first five of a class of 35 had been authorised. Some two years later, in the course of another address, this time to the British Association for the Advancement of Science, Oliver Bulleid released some advance information on the twelve-wheeled tank locomotive, to be known as the 'Leader' class, the first of which was nearing completion at Brighton Works. In the interim, the Southern Railway had been absorbed into the new nationalised system and Bulleid was designated the Chief Mechanical Engineer of the Southern Region of British Railways. There was much work, Bulleid said, for which tender engines were not necessary; to cover such duties – and indeed to meet practically all requirements – a tank engine was needed that would be able to work passenger and goods trains over all the system, with certain unimportant exceptions.

He listed the desirable features of this new tank engine as follows:

1. To be able to run over the majority of the company's lines.
2. To be capable of working all classes of trains up to 90mph.
3. To have its whole weight available for braking and the highest percentage thereof for adhesion.
4. To be equally suitable for running in both directions without turning, with unobstructed lookout.
5. To be ready for service at short notice.
6. To be almost continuously available.
7. To be suitable for complete "common use".
8. To run not less than 100000 miles between general overhauls with little or no attention at the running sheds.
9. To cause minimum wear and tear to the track.
10. To use substantially less fuel and water per drawbar horsepower developed.

Below:
'Leader' class 0-6-6-0T, showing fireman's side. The boiler was offset to allow a corridor to run between the driving cab at the smokebox end and the fireman's compartment amidships.

3 CYL^{RS} PER BOGIE (12$\frac{1}{4}$" DIA X 15" STROKE)

BP 280 LB PER SQ IN.

COAL 4 TONS

WATER 4000 GALL^S

9' 4"

N^{O}1 END

5' 1" DIA

THERMIC SYPHONS

5' 1" DIA

CHAIN DRIVE

N^O

8' 6" — 8' 0" — 7' 6" — 19' 0" — 7' 6" — 8' 0" — 8' 6"

15' 6" — 15' 6"

50' 0 TOTAL WHEELBASE

67' 0" OVERALL

21T. 15C   21T. 15C   21T. 15C   21T. 15C   21T. 15C   21T. 15C

65T 5C   WT IN WORKING ORDER 130T 10C   65T 5C

Various preliminary schemes preceded the final concept, including two tank engines based upon the Q1 goods engine, one an 0–6–2T, the other an 0–6–4T. There was even a proposal for a massive 4–6–4T, but by 1946 the double-ended 0–6–6–OT design was approved in principle. In retrospect it seems remarkable that Bulleid should have succeeded in convincing the Southern Railway management that such a large and indeed revolutionary steam locomotive was the answer to this traffic requirement – which was, in fact, initially supposed to replace a variety of elderly, modestly sized tank engines, such as the M7 0–4–4T. Of course, the one significant difference lay in the idea that a single locomotive could perform the whole range of duties, from branch line to main line, whereas in

Above:
A new design of cylinder, which incorporated a sleeve valve, was produced by Bulleid for the 'Leader' class 0-6-6-0T, and in order to test this in service he chose ex-LBSCR Class H1 4-4-2 No 2039 *Hartland Point* as a partial guineapig. This locomotive was modified in September 1947 with fabricated steel cylinders and sleeve valves operated by levers, chain-driven by sprockets attached at the centre of the driving axle. The front end was cut away and a plain chimney was provided, whilst the leading bogie was replaced by one from a Billinton 'D3' 0-4-4T, with 3ft diameter wheels. Renumbered 32039 by British Railways, the adulterated Atlantic is seen here at Brighton Works in 1949, with 'Leader' class No 36001 in the background. Water consumption of No 32039 in modified form was prolific indeed. *P. F. Winding*

Above:

Seen at Eastleigh in February 1951, in store prior to withdrawal from service. No 32039 *Hartland Point* was finally withdrawn a few weeks later. The modifications for the sleeve valve experiments certainly ruined the graceful lines of the Brighton Atlantic. *L. Elsey*

Above right:

No 36001 at Lewes on 31 August, 1949 running bunker-first on a trial from Brighton to Crowborough. As usual, the fireman has both the door and window wide open in an attempt to keep a reasonable working temperature in the confined working space. The Locomen's representatives were not satisfied with the working conditions of the enginemen and only agreed to a volunteer crew operating No 36001, making it clear that they would require very considerable improvement in working conditions before the class entered service. Bulleid had envisaged oil-firing, which would have eased the problem, but there was also dissatisfaction at the remote location of the fireman's compartment, a feature which would have been more difficult to overcome without drastic redesign. *C. C. B. Herbert*

the past the two concepts were considered separately. To achieve this aim with steam traction would, he believed, require a type of locomotive quite unlike anything hitherto produced in Britain. Bulleid's own Light Pacifics had an admirable route availability, and a Class 7 power rating, but they did not answer to the more idealistic requirements he had set himself, in particular, the availability and freedom from routine shed maintenance. Nor did they have the maximum braking and adhesion factors that he envisaged.

The new 'Leader' class was intended to be a standard type, roughly equivalent in power to a Class 5 mixed-traffic engine, which together with the two Pacific classes could answer all needs other than those where electrification or dieselisation were viable propositions. Because so many new features were proposed, Bulleid sought and obtained authority to build five locomotives, rather than a single prototype, to be tried out in all classes of traffic over Southern metals.

I have already referred to the basic concept of the design, which was an 0–6–6–0T. The underframe was 65ft long and carried the boiler; smokebox, bunker for 4 tons of coal and tank for 4000gal of water, a driving cab at each end and a fireman's cab between the boiler and the bunker. All this was enclosed within an overall casing of rather angular aspect which had no pretentions towards either air-smoothing or streamlining.

The conventional boiler, which had a pressure of 280lb psi, was of modified design in so far as the side and back water spaces of the firebox were replaced by plain sheet steel lined with refractory material; four thermic syphons joined the crown of the firebox to the underside of the barrel. The idea was to avoid the maintenance associated with stayed firebox water spaces. In service this proved a troublesome feature, providing an overheated area which – apart from anything else – made the fireman's job intolerable.

The idea of providing a true mixed-traffic engine depended very much upon keeping the weight down, without sacrificing adhesion and brake power. The calculated tractive effort, at 85 per cent of working pressure, was 26 350lb, roughly equivalent to that of a conventional BR Class 5 locomotive. To meet requirement No. 1

on the list weight had to be kept down to $112\frac{1}{2}$ tons in full working order (an axleload of $19\frac{3}{4}$ tons.) In retrospect it seems odd that Bulleid should have attempted this with such a large locomotive when he already had a Class 7 Pacific (the 'West Country'/'Battle of Britain') which was light enough to work over most secondary routes. Only the more obscure branch lines were barred to the Light Pacifics, and these were worked by a variety of vintage tank engines of modest size and power. A problem which would have prevented the 'Leader' class (at least in its prototype form), from taking over these branch line duties was that it was proved to be far in excess of the heaviest permitted axle-load, whilst the power Class 5 meant that it would have a difficult task matching up to the excellent performances of the Light Pacifics when working over main lines.

The 'Leader' had Bulleid-Walschaerts valve gear operating sleeve valves with rotatory motion to equalise wear (as in internal combustion engine practice) with three fabricated steel cylinders per bogie. Cylinder bore was $12\frac{1}{4}$ in and the stroke was 15in; the wheel

Below:
Only the pioneer locomotive No 36001, ever ran in steam, but never in revenue-earning service, being confined to trial runs, either light engine or hauling empty stock. The livery was shop grey with black lining and cream Gill Sans lettering. The pale patch of paintwork in the centre of the bodyside obliterated the BR lion and wheel emblem, with number below, which the locomotive briefly displayed when new. Steam can be seen issuing from the turbo-generator for the electric lighting, located between the first and second axles. *S. C. Nash*

Below right:
Project abandoned. Uncompleted locomotive No 36003 had been towed to Bognor Regis motive power depot for storage, pending dismantling; previously it had been stored at New Cross Gate. The partial exposure of the leading bogie shows the arrangement of the springs for the three BFB wheels and the sprockets for the chain-drive. The smokebox end of the boiler is visible. Photographed on 10 April, 1950 with the steam from 'Battle of Britain' 4-6-2 No 34069 *Hawkinge* standing on the adjacent track. The order to cease work on the construction of Nos. 36002-5 was given on 19 November, 1949, with No 36002 only two days from completion and No 36003 partially erected (as seen). Tests with No 36001 continued for a further year, with the locomotive transferred to Eastleigh works. *S. C. Nash*

diameter was 5ft 1in. The centre axle was a three-throw crank and there was a chain sprocket at each end, outside the wheels. The outer and inner axles were plain, each having a sprocket at opposite ends, and chains replaced conventional coupling rods – providing an unsymmetrical drive from the centre axle, a feature which later proved a cause of crank axle failures. The bogies had all their working parts enclosed in oil baths and were designed in such a way that they could be removed and interchanged, much in the manner adopted for electric traction.

The dawn of nationalisation saw work well in hand on the design, but Bulleid realised he was now involved in a race against time, because the new regime favoured more simplistic forms of steam locomotive development. No 36001 was completed at Brighton in June 1949 and commenced trial runs on 22 June. Teething troubles were plentiful and really only to be expected, but Bulleid was now 68 years old, and he left the Southern, and his protégé, to take up the post of Consulting Engineer to the CIE in the autumn. The new locomotive was now in the hands of BR, and so troublesome was it proving to be that an order was given on 19 November 1949 to stop work on the next four locomotives in Brighton erecting shop. At this time No

36002 was just two days from completion and No 36003 was reasonably advanced.

Trials with No 36001 continued, but by June 1950 the locomotive had proved so far from serviceable that a last chance was given, with its transfer to Eastleigh where, it was hoped, the staff would have more success with it. A testing crew from York was sent, together with the ex-North Eastern Railway dynamometer car, for a series of trial runs which it was planned No 36001 should to work over the South Western main line between Eastleigh and Woking. For comparative purposes, the locomotive would haul a train of empty stock for a fortnight, with a Maunsell U class 2–6–0 working the same load the following fortnight.

A principal objection to the design was the inadequate and unbearably hot accommodation provided for the fireman, who was forced to wear protective sacking over his legs. Oil-firing would have reduced the discomfort, but it would not have removed the other objection – namely that he was in solitary confinement, out of immediate contact with the driver in the event of an emergency. The trials were not a success; there was trouble with the firebox and the engine was steaming badly. The crank axles broke and were replaced by axles from No 36002, but these broke also.

Weighbridge readings revealed the excess weight plus a disparity of wheel weight between one side and the other. A solution was sought by placing ballast weights down the side corridor, but this of course increased the overall weight of the locomotive still further. It is believed to have been somewhere in the region of 130tons.

In November 1950 the order came to cease work on No 36001; all tests were to stop and the other four uncompleted engines were to be scrapped. The locomotive was left in the open at Eastleigh, before final dismantling took place in 1951.

The engines were built as follows:

No 36001	Brighton	1949
No 36002*	Brighton	1949
Nos 36003-36005**	Brighton	1949

*Withdrawn when virtually completed, November 1949.
**Withdrawn whilst in course of erection, November 1949 (Nos 36002/3 were stored at New Cross Gate in 1949)
Entire class condemned, November 1950.

Left:
Close-up of the front end of 'Leader' No 36001, showing the three cylinders located between the bogie frames, also the extension hoses from cab to bufferbeam for the vacuum brake and steam heating. The centre window opened outwards, the whistle was located above the right-hand window. Photographed at Eastleigh works on 1 October 1950. *L. Elsey*

Above:
'Leader' class 0-6-6-0T No 36001 is seen being dismantled in Eastleigh works, following the BR decision to abandon the project, in 1951. The last trial run was on 2 November 1950, when the persistent teething troubles showed no signs of easing and the locomotive was condemned. Weighbridge readings had earlier revealed that the locomotive was far in excess of the permitted axle load and also had a disparity of weight between one side and the other, largely due to the offset boiler. As a result, the weight of No 36001 had been further increased by the insertion of cast iron ballast in the side corridor, in order to effect a balance. This interesting photograph reveals the side corridor (complete with ballast weights) with the smokebox end of the locomotive nearest the camera. The fireman's compartment is visible amidships, with the bunker and water tank beyond. Bulleid had intended that the bogies should be removable en bloc for overhaul or repair, in a similar manner to the power bogies of electric stock. A shortcoming of the design was the need to remove large portions of the outer body casing in order to reach the boiler, etc, during examination or repair. Even the routine maintenance procedures for a steam locomotive – boiler washout, smokebox cleaning, and so on – were made difficult by the outer superstructure. *S. C. Townroe*

SECTION 5

0–6–6–OT
Mixed-Traffic Engine
Introduced: 1957
Total: 1
'Turf Burner'
Córas Iompair Eireann (CIE)

In a country which had to import almost all of its coal for steam traction, the existence of vast amounts of fuel in the form of peat, or turf, quickly attracted Bulleid to the idea of producing a locomotive design which could burn the native fuel. The disadvantages of turf were already well known to CIE, as various experiments had been made in the past. In particular it had a lower calorific value than coal and a greater quantity was required to produce the same heat output – roughly four times the volume in fact. Thus a greater quantity of ash resulted and the locomotive had to haul a tender of considerably larger capacity if enough fuel was to be carried. The second World War had seen a fuel famine on Eire's railways and despite the known problems turf was used, in the form of briquettes, as well as other lower grade fuels, down to anthracite dust. Even after the war the country was hit by a severe coal shortage (in 1947) and this time CIE used oil-burning apparatus to keep its steam locomotives in limited service. Of course, oil was also an imported fuel and there was no guarantee that similar shortages would not arise (as indeed they did) in the future. If a really successful turf-burning design could be pro-

duced, the fuel problems of CIE, in cases of national shortage, would be considerably reduced and this would allow them to operate a more adequate service. Even the final decision to dieselise the CIE motive power fleet did not deter Bulleid from his objective, as the 'Turf Burner' would be a standby for oil shortages, as well as being suitable power for the seasonal sugar-beet traffic – but that is to run ahead of the evolving story.

When O. V. S. Bulleid left the Southern Region of British Railways to take up his post with the CIE, he went straight to a railway which still operated a fleet of steam locomotives of high average age and of very mixed parentage. The CIE Board had rejected the idea of electrification because of the low density of the population, but had initiated limited use of diesel-electric traction, in the form of five shunting engines and two larger mixed-traffic locomotives. When Bulleid first outlined his ideas for future CIE traction he remained in favour of steam, using imported coal, rather than diesels using imported oil. The ideal – a turf burning steam locomotive – was already in his mind, but only in vague outline. For the moment he thought that a considerable reduction in the aged fleet of steam locomotives was essential; a new standard mixed-traffic design (probably a medium-powered 0–6–0 tank engine) should take their place.

By 1951 it was becoming clear that Bulleid's desire to retain steam was not meeting with the approval of the Government partly due to the ever-increasing cost of imported coal. The CIE Board again considered a switch to diesel traction, although Bulleid was by now able to announce that some progress was being made with experiments with turf as a fuel. Diesel traction was, however, introduced in the form of railcars the same year, and by 1953 the CIE was committed to a programme of dieselisation. As already mentioned, Bulleid was not deterred by this, and in fact he gained authority to build fifty new steam locomotives, burning either turf or oil to supplement the new diesel fleet in periods of peak traffic.

The beginnings of the 'Turf Burner' project are traceable to about 1950. One early proposal was for a compression ignition engine, and there were also thoughts of using pulverised turf. Just as he had done when working on the 'Leader' design, Bulleid selected an existing locomotive to act as a guinea-pig. This was a 1907 Coey inside-cylinder 2–6–0, No 356. A new tender, using parts of an existing ex-Midland Great Western tender was provided, with greater fuel capacity and mounted upon lengthened frames. Behind the tender was coupled a four-wheel wagon, upon which was mounted a diesel-powered blower,

Above:
Once again, as with the 'Leader', Bulleid selected an existing locomotive to act as a guinea-pig for his new ideas, this time an inside-cylinder 2-6-0, No 356. Conversion involved the fitting of a pair of preheating boilers alongside the existing boiler (one each side) and the provision of a mechanical stoker. A Franco-Crosti scheme was considered for this locomotive at one stage. The tender was rebuilt from an existing ex-MGWR tender. The chimney on the smokebox was provided for lighting-up purposes only, the real chimney was at the rear of the tender. The livery was aluminium and the tender was inscribed 'CIE Experimental Turf Burning Locomotive'.
T. K. Widd

Left:
The drawing shows the turf-burning locomotive in its final form, with smoke deflectors added.

which created a draught. The locomotive was fitted with a pair of preheating boilers, each side of the boiler proper, and the flue gases and exhaust steam were used to preheat the boiler feed water in both the preheaters and in the tender, before being allowed to pass into the at-

75

Left:
Running light engine, on trial from Inchicore, No CCI had rather primitive smoke-deflectors added by the time this picture was taken. Judging by the way the exhaust is clearing the drivers' lookout, these were effective in service. They were later improved in shape, as shown in a following illustration. The large fuel hopper and the water tank were duplicated at each end of the locomotive. No electric lights were fitted, and the locomotive carried conventional oil lamp headcodes. *J. G. Click*

Above:
Still in workshop grey livery, No CCI is seen here at the head of some very mixed empty rolling stock during a trial run, at Sallins on 5 September 1957. The engine is in as-built condition. Trouble was experienced with spark throwing, on one occasion setting light to the roof of one of the elderly wooden carriages of the test train. Speeds of up to 70 mph were achieved on these test runs and the locomotive was reported to run as smoothly as a carriage. The draught was provided by fans, driven by turbines, and these gave the engine the advantage of being able to restore steam pressure very quickly after being worked hard. Before being exhausted through two chimneys, one each end of the cabs, the hot gases of combustion were led past feed water heaters. *J. G. Click*

mosphere through a chimney at the rear of the tender. Between 1952 and 1954 a series of trials and modifications took place with No 356 including, latterly, a venture onto the main line which ended in total failure at Cork.

Valuable lessons were learned from the experimental engine, which in itself was not considered a success. Once again – as so often in Bulleid's career – the sands of time were running out, and once again his remarkable powers of persuasion won the day. As mentioned earlier he sought, and gained, authority to proceed with the turf burning project despite a CIE decision to dieselise. His ideas had by now taken more definite form, and the layout of his new engine was clearly influenced by his final design for the Southern – the highly controversial 'Leader' class – in so far as it was to be an 0–6–6–0 double bogie tank engine. The boiler was in fact proportioned for oil fuel, but was also suitable for turf at a more restricted power output. Two mechanical stokers fed the crushed turf from the two fuel hoppers to the firebox, where it was spread by steam jets. Draughting was provided by a fan at each end of the locomotive, with the exhaust gases being discharged through chimneys in front of each cab. At the base of both chimneys there was a spark-arresting device, intended to deflect sparks back into the firebox. The cabs themselves were arranged, one for each direction of travel, and had a door only on the left-hand side facing the direction of travel; the cabs were located between the fuel bunkers and the central boilers and firebox.

The bogies were self-contained units, as in the 'Leader' class, and each had a two-cylinder steam engine with enclosed crankshaft and oil bath lubrication. External coupling of the axles was by means of chains, totally enclosed. The bogie wheel diameter was 3ft 7in, compared to 5ft 1in for the 'Leader,' and the drawgear and buffers were conventionally placed at the ends of the massive underframe, and not upon the bogies, as featured in the 'Leader' design. Each bogie had two brake cylinders. In reality the 'Turf Burner' was a very different locomotive to the 'Leader', and it was also considerably smaller and less powerful. It was only 60ft long, compared to 76ft and the tractive effort was 19926lb compared to 26300lb. The square boiler had 250lb psi pressure. The entire layout was different, with a centralised firebox and two outer ends which duplicated all essential items, whereas the 'Leader' had conformed more to a normal locomotive layout, except for the location of the cabs at each end.

The locomotive was numbered CCI, in true Bulleid style, and was steamed at Inchicore in August 1957, making its first movements in steam in the works yard. Once out on the main line it displayed a tendency to throw sparks, but ran with remarkable quietness, soon earning the nickname of "the quiet one". Line tests were certainly more satisfactory than had been the case with the 'Leader', and one suspects that Bulleid had been successful in ironing out a lot of the problems he had encountered with his first 0–6–6–0T design. But although he demonstrated a considerable measure of technical success with No CC1 he was never to see the design become accepted and multiplied; yet again time had run out. In May 1958 he retired from his post of Chief Mechanical Engineer of the CIE. The locomotive was never tried out as an oil-burner (as Bulleid had intended should happen once he had proved its suitability for turf burning) and it had never run in revenue-earning service. By this time the CIE diesel programme was well under way and the locomotive was quietly placed in a siding at Inchicore. There it remained, cold and neglected, until 1965, a sad end to the last steam locomotive design by O. V. S. Bulleid and the last steam locomotive design produced for Ireland. The plan to build fifty was quietly forgotten – the diesel had won the day.

The engine was built as follows:

Far left:
No CCI, the 'Turf Burner' in final form, with smoke-deflectors added to the ends and painted bright green with yellow 'dazzle' stripes, lining and lettering. The 'dazzle' effect was added because the locomotive was extremely silent when running, soon earning the nickname of 'the quiet one'. A chime whistle was fitted and frequently used to warn of the engine's approach. The photograph was taken in the works yard at Inchicore, on 3 June 1961, with the project shelved, although the engine survived intact until 1965. It only worked a total of some 2,000 miles all told, and never entered revenue-earning service. *S. C. Nash*

No CC1   Inchicore   1957

Withdrawal: 1965
Nominal (Never placed in CIE stock.)

The BR Rebuilds

The decision to modify the Bulleid Pacifics was finally taken in 1955. Compared to their counterparts on other Regions they were not wholly efficient engines and were heavy on oil and coal. Design proposals for a comprehensive modification of the 'Merchant Navy' class began to take shape at Brighton in 1954. The entire class was subsequently rebuilt, together with all but 50 of the 'West Country' and 'Battle of Britain' engines between 1956-61. With the writing already on the wall for steam traction in Britain, the careers of these rebuilt Pacifics were tragically short. R. G. Jarvis was in charge of the design work at Brighton and is quoted as saying that the engines remained 90 per cent Bulleid, even if they had lost the features to which he was specially attached.

In fact, Bulleid is known to have disliked the changes, but he would probably have accepted them in due course because they certainly produced one of the finest of all British Pacific locomotive designs both in terms of performance and appearance.

4-6-2 Class 8P
Express Passenger Engines
(BR rebuild of Bulleid MN class)
Introduced: 1956
Total: 30
Modified 'Merchant Navy'

In 1955 authority was given for the rebuilding of 15 out of the 30 'Merchant Navy' class Pacifics, together with 15 of the Light Pacifics. The 'Merchant Navy' was tackled first, and in the early weeks of 1956 Eastleigh released No 35018 *British India Line* in modified form. Visually there was a distinct family likeness to the Riddles BR standard engines, although the distinctive Bulleid wheels were retained. The whole air-smoothed casing was removed and boiler clothing of conventional type was used instead, allowing ease of access and maintenance. Large smoke-deflectors were fitted, and the multiple-jet chimney had a pleasing form in cast iron. The original boiler was retained, at the lower pressure of 250lb psi, but a new saddle-supported cylindrical smokebox was fitted, using the original door.

The firegrate had a manually-operated rocking section in two parts and there were modifications to the triple ashpan of the original engines. A new superheater header was fitted and outside steampipes fed the two outside cylinders. The mechanical lubricators for the cylinders and valve chests were relocated on the running plate, instead of their original position beneath the smokebox frontplate (where they had been vulnerable to fire ash when the smokebox was cleaned). A new

Below:
Modified 'Merchant Navy' Pacific, as reconstructed at Eastleigh, 1956-59, with 6,000gal tender.

lubricator was provided for the slidebars and coupled axleboxes, replacing the multi-feed oil boxes in the cab. All the lubricators were driven from the expansion links of the outside valve motion.

The troublesome oil bath and chain-driven Bulleid valve gear was removed entirely, and three separate sets of Walschaerts valve motion were used; those for the outside cylinders were driven by return cranks placed on the driving crankpins, and by crosshead arms attached to the crossheads. The inside valve gear was driven by an eccentric mounted on the right-hand crank web of the driving axle. Maximum valve travel was $6\frac{3}{4}$in for the outside

Above:
The first 'Merchant Navy' to undergo modification was No 35018 *British India Line*, which appeared from Eastleigh early in 1956. A new saddle-supported cylindrical smokebox was provided, but the unique Bulleid smokebox door was retained. This view of No 35018 approaching completion suggests that they would have been exceedingly handsome engines minus the smoke deflectors. Three sets of Walschaerts valve gear replaced the unique and troublesome Bulleid chain-driven motion. The boiler was retained, at the lower pressure of 250lb psi introduced to the original engines by Jarvis in 1952. The layout of the sanding gear was revised for both the 'Merchant Navy' class and the Light Pacifics in their modified form, as explained in detail on page 95. *British Rail SR*

valves and $6\frac{1}{4}$in for the inside valve. The steam reversing gear originally fitted was dispensed with and replaced by screw gear, with a cut-off indicator of the drum type. A single reversing shaft was fitted for the three valve gears, operated by slide blocks in the radius rod, a design developed on the LMS by Ivatt.

A new inside cylinder, with inside admission piston valves, and the steamchest offset to the right, formed part of the smokebox saddle together with a fabricated stretcher, which was attached to the main frames. Because the existing outside cylinders were retained, with their outside admission, the drive of the valve stem of the new piston valves was taken from the top pin of the combustion lever, instead of the second pin. In place of the usual valve-spindle crosshead, a suspension link supported this part of the gear. The original piston rod and crosshead were a single forging, and these were replaced by a separate crosshead with the normal cone and cotter attachment.

The cab structure remained unaltered, except that the lower portion of the curved side sheeting was cut away, partly to increase

Above:
Pacific transformed. The first appearance of No 35018 *British India Line* at Waterloo was on 14 February 1956, when it was officially inspected. By the time this picture was taken, on Easter Day the same year, handrails had been added to the smoke deflectors. The engine is seen leaving on the 'Bournemouth Belle'.
F. Spencer Yeates

Right:
Close-up of the clever adaptation of the existing outside cylinders to take the Walschaerts valve gear. This also shows the location of mechanical lubricators and the new sandbox for the leading coupled wheels. The Bulleid clasp brakes are retained and balance weights have been added to the BFB coupled wheels. This official photograph was taken prior to the decision to fit handrails to the smoke deflectors.
British Rail SR

Above:
The second engine to be modified was No 35020 *Bibby Line*, which emerged from Eastleigh in April 1956. For some weeks it ran with an unmodified 6,000gal tender, as seen here, and this certainly gave a more massive appearance to the ensemble. No 35020 was selected for tests to prove the worth of the redesign, and undertook controlled road tests, as well as service tests, on the Waterloo-Salisbury Exeter route. The engine was photographed during trials on the WR, with the Swindon Dynamometer Car behind the tender; which was specially fitted for these trials, and borrowed from No 35028. *British Rail*

accessibility and partly for appearance. A foothole was cut into the lower portion of the cab side and the original cab roof ventilator was replaced by a new one supported on links. Provision of the screw-operated reversing gear involved moving the driver's seat back slightly. The Ajax type firehole door was retained, but without the steam-operating gear, and a deflector plate was added to improve combustion.

Modification of the Pacifics tenders in fact preceded the engines by some three years or so, and was sufficiently under way for a number of locomotives to run with modified tenders in their original Bulleid form (see page 35.) The modification involved the removal of the side raves and the provision of compartments for the fireirons on either side of the bunker. The rear of the tender top was flat and a protective casing was placed over the vacuum reservoirs. All the existing MN tenders were so treated and nine of the smaller tenders received new 5250gal bodies on the original frames; these were used on both the 'Merchant Navy' and the Light Pacifics. The weight in working order of a rebuilt 6000gal tender was given as 53.6tons, and the engine weighed 97.9tons in full working order in the rebuilt form.

The engines were rebuilt as follows:

No 35001	Eastleigh	8/1959
No 35002	Eastleigh	5/1958
No 35003	Eastleigh	9/1959
No 35004	Eastleigh	7/1958
No 35005	Eastleigh	6/1959
No 35006	Eastleigh	10/1959
No 35007	Eastleigh	5/1958
No 35008	Eastleigh	5/1957
No 35009	Eastleigh	3/1957
No 35010	Eastleigh	1/1957
No 35011	Eastleigh	7/1959
No 35012	Eastleigh	2/1957
No 35013	Eastleigh	5/1956
No 35014	Eastleigh	7/1956

Above:
Seen in positively beautiful ex-works conditions, at Eastleigh on 12 March 1964 is No 35029 *Ellerman Lines*, attached to a rebuilt 5,250gal tender off the original batch of 10 engines. It seems scarcely credible that this immaculate piece of machinery was withdrawn from service just two and a half years later. After rusting away at Barry for many years, the engine was later rescued and has now been lovingly restored as a sectioned exhibit at the National Railway Museum, York – a fitting end indeed (see page 116). In addition to the nine 5,250gal tenders with new bodies, there was one 6,000gal re-bodied version; rebuilt from the self-weighing tender. *G. H. Wheeler*

Left:
Attached to No 35014 *Nederland Line,* at Nine Elms shed on 10 September 1966 is one of the 5,250 gal tenders which had new bodies on the existing frames, with externally a rather square appearance. Only one ladder was provided at the rear of these tenders, whereas the larger 6,000gal tenders had two. The locomotive was withdrawn from service just six months later. *P. H. Groom*

Below left:
No 35021 *New Zealand Line,* seen leaving Basingstoke, is attached to one of the modified 6,000gal tenders and the longer wheelbase is very evident in this view, compared to the preceding

illustration. Two ladders are provided at the rear, and the vacuum reservoirs are clearly seen under their protective shield at the rear of the coal space. The removal of the side raves from the Bulleid Pacific tenders had the effect of eliminating pockets where surplus coal tended to accumulate uselessly, as well as facilitating the taking of water. *Alec Swain*

Below:
The rebuilt 'Merchant Navy' Pacifics were undeniably imposing machines, especially when seen in motion. No 35029 *Ellerman Lines* makes a classic study as it races out of Buckhorn Weston Tunnel with the up 'Atlantic Coast Express' on 14 October 1961. *G. A. Richardson*

No 35015	Eastleigh	6/1958
No 35016	Eastleigh	4/1957
No 35017	Eastleigh	3/1957
No 35018	Eastleigh	2/1956
No 35019	Eastleigh	5/1959
No 35020	Eastleigh	4/1956
No 35021	Eastleigh	6/1959
No 35022	Eastleigh	6/1956
No 35023	Eastleigh	2/1957
No 35024	Eastleigh	5/1959
No 35025	Eastleigh	12/1956
No 35026	Eastleigh	1/1957
No 35027	Eastleigh	5/1957
No 35028	Eastleigh	10/1959
No 35029	Eastleigh	9/1959
No 35030	Eastleigh	4/1958

locomotives quickly followed the initial order. In their rebuilt state the 'Merchant Navy' class proved more reliable than the original Bulleid creation, and they were still able to run at high speed when the opportunity presented itself.

Because the total withdrawal of steam traction was already well under way by the time the last engines had been rebuilt, they did not attain high mileages before withdrawals commenced in 1964, with only a few exceeding one million miles since building in their original Bulleid form.

First of Class Withdrawn: 35002/15 (1964)
Last of Class Withdrawn: 35003/7/8/23/28/30 (1967)

It can be seen from the dates given above that authority to rebuild the remaining 15

Top:
Beautifully groomed for an enthusiast special No 35026 *Lamport and Holt Line* positively sparkles in this classic example of night photography, taken as the engine stands in the yard at Stockport Edgeley motive power depot. The balance weights added to the Bulleid-Firth-Brown driving wheels are particularly well illuminated, together with the clasp brake gear for the coupled wheels. The engine is attached to one of the rebodied 5,250gal tenders. *J. R. Carter*

Above:
No 35017 *Belgian Marine* standing in the carriage sidings at Clapham Junction. The imposing appearance of the rebuilt Bulleid Pacifics perhaps surpassed that of the BR standard engines which they resembled. In particular, the large-diameter chimney was very successfully shaped in the BR idiom, and the running plate (which was attached by brackets to the main frames, as opposed to the boiler) was at just the right height to give a balanced appearance to the engine, from whichever angle it was viewed. In this rear ¾ view the layout of the injectors, on the fireman's side, and the unusual location of the whistle on the boiler are particularly well illustrated. *Author*

Above:

It was the replacement of steam by electric and diesel traction that was to sound the death knell of the rebuilt Bulleid 'Merchant Navy' Pacifics whilst still young and in fine fettle, and once it was realised that their days were numbered a variety of special railtours was organised by enthusiast societies. Nonetheless their everyday routine rosters also began to attract numerous photographers and recorders. The 1960s witnessed the Bulleid engines receiving more attention, and enthusiastic devotion, than at any previous time in their BR, and before that, SR careers. Happily many fine photographs were taken, before it was too late; such as this attractive study of No 35023 *Holland-Afrika Line* taking water at Southampton Central, whilst working a Bournemouth-Waterloo express on 2 June 1962. *J. R. Woolley*

Above:

With nameplates and smokebox numberplate removed, No 35008 (formerly *Orient Line*) still makes a proud spectacle at Nine Elms on 3 May 1967 although withdrawn from service only two months later, when all the remaining Pacifics were made redundant. These were hectic days for the rail enthusiast – a final fling before the last steam worked main line services in Britain gave away to modernisation. The Pacifics themselves were far from life-expired, but no further use could be found for them.   *J. Scrace*

Right:

No 35023 (formerly *Holland-Afrika Line*) had the dubious honour of powering the last steam working from Waterloo prior to complete electrification and dieselisation. This was the 8.30am Waterloo-Weymouth on 9 July 1967, seen here passing through Farnborough station. The engine was chosen because of a reputation it had gained for very fast running in the final days of steam. The same day as this photograph was taken, the remaining 'Merchant Navy' locomotives were withdrawn for scrap, these were Nos 35003/7/8/23/28/30.
G. P. Cooper

4–6–2 Class 7P5F
Passenger Engines
(BR rebuild of Bulleid WC and BB class
Light Pacifics)
Introduced: 1957
Total: 60
Modified 'West Country' and 'Battle of Britain'

The first of the Light Pacifics to undergo modification was No 34005 *Barnstaple*, which appeared in the summer of 1957. The general effect was to produce a very similar locomotive to the modified 'Merchant Navy' class, and the technical changes are as detailed in the previous section (pages 78-89). One alteration was the widening of the cabs from 8ft 6in to 9ft for those locomotives which formerly had the

Below:
The appearance of the rebuilt Light Pacifics closely followed that evolved for the 'Merchant Navy' class. One difference was the siting of the nameplates, which on the small engines were attached to a backplate bracketed to the running plate, whereas the 'Merchant Navy' nameplates were attached to the boiler sides. Rebuilt 'West Country' No 34017 *Ilfracombe* makes a fine study as she heads westward out of Salisbury with a Saturday extra, on 27 July 1963. Unlike their contemporary BR standard counterparts, the rebuilt Bulleid engines retained the electric lighting of the originals, a much-appreciated feature which was somewhat surprisingly not adopted by Riddles for his own Pacifics. *A. Richardson*

Top:
A striking view of rebuilt 'West Country' Pacific No 34013 *Okehampton,* panned by the camera as the locomotive speeds through Drayton, near Chichester, with a Locomotive Club of Great Britain 'Isle of Wight Farewell Tour' special. The work of rebuilding the Light Pacifics began in 1957 (No 34005 *Barnstaple* was the first to appear from Eastleigh) and continued for four years, less a few days, by which time 60 engines had been dealt with. *David Hill*

Above:
The rebuilt 'Battle of Britain' engines also had the position of the plaques and nameplates reversed, with the plaque now above the name in the same style as on the rebuilt 'West Country' Pacifics. No 34056 *Croydon* is particularly attractive in ex-works condition, at Eastleigh in October 1962. *G. Wheeler*

Above:
Rebuilt 'Battle of Britain' class 4-6-2 No 34087 *145 Squadron* is seen here at Nine Elms (minus nameplates), in one of the final weeks of SR steam activity. The tender attached is one of the newer 5,250 gal capacity type with a new body, of cleaner outlines, mounted upon the original underframes. These new bodies replaced examples which had become very badly corroded since construction. *J. Welland*

Above right:
With exhaust playing around the top of the smokebox. No 34090 *Sir Eustace Missenden, Southern Railway* races downhill towards Buckhorn Weston Tunnel, near Templecombe, with the 8.35 (SO) Waterloo to Exeter train on 7 September 1963. The engine retained its uniquely shaped nameplates upon rebuilding. A 4,500gal tender was attached and the reduced width, to suit the Hastings line gauge, is very evident in this picture, compared to the engine and the leading carriage. *A. Richardson*

Right:
A driver admires the cabside 'long service' plaque presented by the Royal Observer Corps, for No 34050, which carried their name; 25 July 1961. *British Rail*

Hastings gauge cab (see page 45) but other detail changes for the engines and for the tenders were as for the larger engines. One effect of the modification was to increase the engine weight to 90tons 1cwt in working order, compared to 86tons for the original design, which resulted in some route restrictions for the modified engines. In particular they were never allowed to Barnstaple, Ilfracombe or Padstow.

The rebuilding, which was initially authorised for 15 locomotives, extended to 60 examples before being brought to a halt. By this time (1961) the cost could no longer be justified and the remaining 50 engines worked out their lives in original form. No 34104 *Bere Alston* was the last to be modified in May 1961, and only lasted six years in this form before withdrawal.

The engines which were rebuilt were as follows:

Modified 'West Country' class

No 34001	Eastleigh	11/1957
No 34003	Eastleigh	9/1957
No 34004	Eastleigh	2/1958

No 34005	Eastleigh	6/1957
No 34008	Eastleigh	6/1960
No 34009	Eastleigh	1/1961
No 34010	Eastleigh	1/1959
No 34012	Eastleigh	1/1958
No 34013	Eastleigh	10/1957
No 34014	Eastleigh	3/1958
No 34016	Eastleigh	4/1958
No 34017	Eastleigh	11/1957
No 34018	Eastleigh	9/1958
No 34021	Eastleigh	12/1957
No 34022	Eastleigh	12/1957
No 34024	Eastleigh	2/1961
No 34025	Eastleigh	10/1957
No 34026	Eastleigh	2/1958
No 34027	Eastleigh	9/1957
No 34028	Eastleigh	8/1958
No 34029	Eastleigh	12/1958
No 34031	Eastleigh	11/1958
No 34032	Eastleigh	10/1960
No 34034	Eastleigh	8/1960
No 34036	Eastleigh	8/1960
No 34037	Eastleigh	3/1958
No 34039	Eastleigh	1/1959
No 34040	Eastleigh	10/1960

No 34042	Eastleigh	1/1959
No 34044	Eastleigh	5/1960
No 34045	Eastleigh	10/1958
No 34046	Eastleigh	2/1959
No 34047	Eastleigh	11/1958
No 34048	Eastleigh	3/1959
No 34093	Eastleigh	5/1960
No 34095	Eastleigh	1/1961
No 34096	Eastleigh	4/1961
No 34097	Eastleigh	2/1961
No 34098	Eastleigh	2/1961
No 34100	Eastleigh	9/1960
No 34101	Eastleigh	9/1960
No 34104	Eastleigh	5/1961
No 34108	Eastleigh	4/1961

Modified 'Battle of Britain' class

No 34050	Eastleigh	8/1958
No 34052	Eastleigh	9/1958
No 34053	Eastleigh	11/1958
No 34056	Eastleigh	12/1960
No 34058	Eastleigh	11/1960
No 34059	Eastleigh	3/1960
No 34060	Eastleigh	11/1960
No 34062	Eastleigh	3/1960
No 34071	Eastleigh	5/1960
No 34077	Eastleigh	7/1960
No 34082	Eastleigh	4/1960
No 34085	Eastleigh	6/1960
No 34087	Eastleigh	12/1960
No 34088	Eastleigh	4/1960
No 34089	Eastleigh	11/1960
No 34090	Eastleigh	8/1960
No 34109	Eastleigh	3/1961

As in the case of the modified 'Merchant Navy' class locomotives, the layout of the sanding gear was altered, partly because of the removal of the air-smoothed casing. The previous sand–

Left:
With nameplates removed, but still retaining the large backplate, No 34004 (formerly *Yeovil*) heads the 8.46am Bournemouth-Waterloo in Winchfield Cutting, as 'Merchant Navy' No 35030 (formerly *Elder-Dempster Lines*) approaches with the 10.24am (SO) from Waterloo, on Saturday 10 June 1967, only weeks from the end of steam on the Southern.
G. P. Cooper

Above left:
Photographed at Eastleigh shed on 4 June 1967, 'West Country' class 4-6-2 No 34024 (formerly named *Tamar Valley*), gets a 'wash and brush up' – probably its last before withdrawal from service. *G. S. Cocks*

Left:
Rebuilt Light Pacific No 34082 *615 Squadron* under the coaling-plant at Nine Elms MPD. The battery box for the BR AWS system is clearly visible on the front footplate below the smokebox. *Eric Treacy*

Above:
Light Pacific power for the Pullman Car 'Bournemouth Belle' on 18 August 1966. The down train is seen passing New Malden hauled by No 34100 *Appledore*. *J. H. Cooper-Smith*

boxes were replaced by new ones; those for the leading pair of wheels were placed above the footplate adjacent to the back of the smokebox, and those for the driving pair of wheels were between the frames, fed by fillers above the footplate. Steam sanding gear, applied to the leading and driving wheels, was arranged for forward running, but in addition steam sandpipes were provided behind the driving wheels for reverse running; these replaced the gravity sanding gear, which was previously fitted to the front end of the tender for this purpose.

It was rebuild No 34089 *602 Squadron* which had the dubious honour of being the last steam locomotive to be repaired at Eastleigh, leaving the works on 3 October 1966 and remaining in traffic for only another eight months or so, before the final withdrawals took place.

First of (Modified) Class Withdrawn: 34028 (1964)
Last of (Modified) Class Withdrawn: 34001/4/13/18/21/24/25/36/37/52/60/87/89/90/93/95. (1967).

Appendix 1

Electric Locomotives

The Electrical Engineer of the Southern Railway for almost the entire period that O. V. S. Bulleid was the Chief Mechanical Engineer, was Alfred Raworth. Bulleid and Raworth held opposing views on some aspects of the SR electrification programme, but nevertheless they collaborated most successfully on the design and production of three large electric locomotives. Bulleid was responsible for their mechanical portions and their maintenance in service. The external appearance of these locomotives was also influenced by Bulleid's views on aesthetics and function and had the same somewhat austere finish which characterised his multiple-unit electric stock in the 1940/50 period.

Below:
Devoid of lettering or numerals, except for the Bulleid numbering CCl on the bufferbeams, and finished in grey livery with white stripes, the first electric locomotive emerged from Ashford Works in 1941. The box-like body and massive underframe certainly gave a solid look to the locomotive, which was mounted on two six-wheel bogies of Bulleid design with BFB (Bulleid-Firth-Brown) wheels of 3ft 6in diameter. The locomotive weighed 99tons and was 56ft 9in long overall, tractive effort was 40,000lb.   *British Rail SR*

Bottom:
Intended as a mixed traffic type, the electric locomotive had to be capable of bridging the gaps in the conductor rail. This was a necessity when starting away from a station. The solution was found by providing a 'booster' unit in the form of a flywheel-driven generator. No CCl is seen here with a southbound goods working at Merstham on 5 December 1941.   *British Rail SR*

Top:
A second basically similar locomotive, No CC2, emerged from Ashford Works in 1943 with some improvements based on experience in traffic with the prototype. The provision of combined electric headlamps and marker discs and multiple-unit jumper cables made the front ends more businesslike in appearance. No CC2, seen here in postwar Malachite green livery, also displays the pantograph which was fitted to all three locomotives to enable them to operate in goods yards where there was no third-rail. Special tramway-type catenary was designed for such locations. The headcode panel, which was a feature of No CC1, was not fitted to CC2. *British Rail SR*

Above:
The third of the Bulleid/Raworth Co-Co electric locomotives was a more powerful machine with a tractive effort of 45,000lb and increased length and weight of 58ft 3in and 105 tons respectively. The appearance was even more box-like, with a blunt front end style similar to that of the postwar Bulleid electric suburban multiple-units. No 20003 did not appear until after nationalisation, in October 1948, and was finished in Malachite green with Gill Sans numerals and lettering, with yellow lining. When this official photograph was taken, at Lovers Walk Brighton, the roof pantograph had not yet been fitted (see photograph at bottom of page 100). *British Rail SR*

Bottom left:
The early BR livery of black with silver/aluminium roof, bogies and lining, applied circa 1949/50, certainly altered the appearance of Nos CC1/2 (which were renumbered 20001/2) and No 20003, which latter presents a bold face at the head of the Newhaven boat train (in red and cream livery) leaving Victoria on 6 April 1950. The roof well with the pantograph is clearly visible. *British Rail SR*

Below:
An attractive livery of BR locomotive green with red and white lining and pale grey-green frames was applied in the late 1950s, as seen on No 20002, photographed at Eastleigh on 21 July 1959. This locomotive carried an experimental light blue livery for a period in 1948/9, as part of a proposed new BR scheme, and was exhibited to the Railway Executive at Kensington Addison Road Station. *L. Elsey*

Above:
The final livery scheme of BR rail blue, with yellow warning on the front ends and twin air horns on the cab roof. The route indicator headcode panel had been restored to use (and the headlamps removed) on No 20001 in its last years of service, seen here as the locomotive heads a Derby Day Royal Train to Tattenham Corner from Victoria and passes Reedham on 31 May 1968. Despite the immaculate appearance of the locomotive, its days were numbered and, together with No 20002, it was withdrawn in the following December. The last of the trio to be built, No 20003, in fact was the first to go, in October 1968. They were popular and efficient locomotives. *J. Scrace*

Appendix 2

Diesel Locomotives

A brief pictorial review is presented of the diesel locomotive designs which appeared whilst O. V. S. Bulleid was Chief Mechanical Engineer, both in Britain and Eire. His actual involvement in their design varied considerably, although the mechanical portions were under his control and were somewhat influenced by his views on locomotive appearance, as in the case of the SR electrics. In retrospect it is clear that whilst on the SR Bulleid was not over-enthusiastic where diesel power was concerned, but his enthusiasm grew for the massive CIE dieselisation programme in later years. His three SR main line locomotives were nevertheless to have an appreciable influence on the form of the Pilot Scheme diesels of comparable power produced by British Railways.

Right:
Towards the end of 1946 the Southern Railway decided to build three diesel-electric locomotives for express passenger service, and by July 1947 the design of these was under way. Not until 1951, however, did the first unit, No 10201, appear from Ashford Works, well after the retirement of O.V.S. Bulleid. This locomotive, and the second one, had 1,750hp English Electric 16-cylinder diesel engines similar to the 1,600hp version installed in the pioneer LMS mixed traffic Nos 10000/1. (It is worth placing on record that Nos 10201-3 were in fact first considered before the LMS design, but were delayed in authorisation). Six nose-suspended, axle-hung traction motors were provided driving three axles on each bogie. The design of the bogie closely followed that used for the three electric locomotives (see pages 98-101), but had an additional axle, for weight carrying purposes, in the form of a pony truck. Maximum tractive effort was 31,200lb and the weight in working order was 135tons. The fuel oil capacity was 1,150gal. Overall length of the locomotives was 63ft 9in. The black and silver livery at first applied was similar to that introduced by the LMS for their diesel electric Co-Cos.   *British Rail SR*

Above:
Clear Bulleid influence is apparent in the Boxpok wheels of 500 hp diesel-mechanical No 11001. This shunting engine was designed by the Southern but did not appear until after nationalisation, in 1950. It was constructed at Ashford and was powered by a 12-cylinder V-type Paxman engine with a three-speed gearbox. It weighed 49½ tons in full working order and the length was 33ft 3in over buffers. Intended for heavy shunting and short-distance transfer and trip work, No 11001 was transferred to the Leeds area for some time, later returning to the SR which withdrew it after a life of only nine years, in August 1959. Livery was always plain black.   *Ian Allan Library*

Above:
The third of the Bulleid main-line diesel-electrics was rated at 2,000hp and was in some ways the precursor of the Pilot scheme BR Type 4 designs. It was three tons lighter, at 132tons, than Nos 10201/2. The original black and silver livery was later replaced by BR standard locomotive green with orange and black lining and, for some odd reason, a primrose yellow roof, which soon dirtied down. No 10203 was photographed in service on the LMR main line near Tring with a freight, on 24 March 1959. Bulleid shaped the exterior of these diesels to match the profile of his own postwar carriages, and he intended that they should be finished in a matching Malachite green livery. *G. J. Jefferson*

Above:
With air horns perched on the roof in place of the original chime whistle, Nos 10203 and 10201 stand forlorn at Derby in their final state, with yellow warning panels above the bufferbeam. Condemned to a comparatively early withdrawal the Bulleid design nevertheless influenced the first generation BR diesel-electrics, in particular the bogie design which was applied to both the BR Sulzer 'Peak' and the English Electric Type 4. *Ian Allan Library*

Left:
For a period in 1954 the Southern tried out No 10202 on the 'Golden Arrow' and 'Night Ferry' services, the same engine working all four trains each day. The engine is seen here leaving Victoria with the 1.00pm 'Golden Arrow' service to Folkestone – in no way so colourful as the normal Pacific! *British Rail SR*

Above:
Although Bulleid fought for residual use of turf-burning steam locomotives for peak and emergency traffic in the shape of his 'Turf Burner' No CC1 (see page 74), he masterminded the CIE switch to dieselisation for future locomotive construction, and drew up a plan for total conversion. In 1953 tenders were invited from many builders in other countries. Orders were placed with Metropolitan-Vickers for 60 1,200 hp diesel-electric Co-Cos and 34 smaller Bo-Bos (see bottom left). The 1,200 hp design was designated Class A and appeared in 1955. They were fabricated by Metro-Cammell in Birmingham and erected in the former LNER carriage shops at Dukinfield, Manchester, with Crossley engines. *Ian Allan Library*

Centre left:
Delivery of the Class A diesel-electric was completed by January 1957. By the time No A34 was photographed, in August 1959, the original livery had been replaced by a bright green which suited them better. They were not wholly efficient locomotives in their original form and in due course received extensive modifications, including fitting entirely new engines of General Motors design. No A34 was photographed leaving Dundalk with a Dublin bound goods. *Frank Church*

Bottom left:
CIE Class C diesel-electric No C202 stands at Drimoleague (Cork, Bandon and South Coast section) with the 2.20pm from Baltimore, consisting of veteran six-wheelers, on 15 July 1957. The class was designed for secondary and branch line work and had a Bo-Bo wheel arrangement. An order was placed for 34 of these Crossley-engined 550hp locomotives, which were finished in an unexciting metallic silver-grey livery. Chief influence on the appearance was the builder, Metropolitan-Vickers, although Bulleid kept a close watch on design progress, as in the case of the larger Class A and B designs. *C. P. Boocock*

Top:
Some time before Bulleid arrived in Ireland the CIE had ordered 10 Sulzer 950 hp diesel engines. These engines, used in pairs, were intended to power five main line diesel locomotives of 1,900hp. The engines had actually arrived in packing cases at Dublin Docks when the locomotives were cancelled. For some years they lay idle before being utilised in 10 Class B A1A-A1A diesels of 950hp, with bodywork by the Birmingham Railway Carriage & Wagon Co; numbered B101-112. In service they proved more reliable than the A and C class diesels with Crossley engines. Their appearance differed somewhat from the other two classes because of the use of three cab windows of neater proportions. *Ian Allan Library*

Above:
For shunting duties the CIE ordered 19 small diesel-hydraulics, with Maybach engines and Mekydro transmissions, of German origin. Bulleid decided that the CIE could construct the mechanical portions at Inchicore, where assembly of the locomotives took place. These were numbered E401-419 and were completed in 1954. A further 14 locomotives were built at Inchicore in 1961. No E404 is seen approaching Amiens Street, Dublin with a goods on 1 August 1959. *Frank Church*

Appendix 3

Named Locomotives

This list shows all named Bulleid locomotives, with their original numbers and later BR numbers. Locomotives delivered after nationalisation (1948 onwards) are shown in italics.

The original Bulleid numbering scheme was highly unusual and was an adaptation of Continental practice, based on the number of axles on a locomotive, not the wheels. Thus a 4–6–2 was a 21C. The '2' represented two leading carrying axles, i.e. the bogie; the '1' represented one trailing carrying axle, i.e. the truck; and the C represented the three coupled axles (based on A as 1, B as 2, C as 3 etc.) Added to this was the number of each individual locomotive, 21C1 being No 1 of the class, and so on.

Bulleid's nameplates were a particularly attractive feature of his engines, in many cases having a pictorial motif in addition to the lettering, which added colour to their appearance.

In the following lists, locomotives marked with an asterisk (*) are those rebuilt by British Railways.

4–6–2 Class MN BR class 8P
'Merchant Navy' (see page 18 and 78*)

*21C1 *(35001)* Channel Packet
*21C2 *(35002)* Union Castle
*21C3 *(35003)* Royal Mail
*21C4 *(35004)* Cunard White Star
*21C5 *(35005)* Canadian Pacific
*21C6 *(35006)* Peninsular & Oriental S.N. Co.
*21C7 *(35007)* Aberdeen Commonwealth
*21C8 *(35008)* Orient Line
*21C9 *(35009)* Shaw Savill
*21C10 *(35010)* Blue Star
*21C11 *(35011)* General Steam Navigation
*21C12 *(35012)* United States Lines
*21C13 *(35013)* Blue Funnel (1)
*21C14 *(35014)* Nederland Line
*21C15 *(35015)* Rotterdam Lloyd
*21C16 *(35016)* Elders Fyffes
*21C17 *(35017)* Belgian Marine
*21C18 *(35018)* British India Line
*21C19 *(35019)* French Line C.G.T.
*21C20 *(35020)* Bibby Line
**35021* New Zealand Line*
**35022* Holland-America Line*
**35023* Holland-Afrika Line*
**35024* East Asiatic Company*
**35025* Brocklebank Line*
**35026* Lamport & Holt Line*
**35027* Port Line*
**35028* Clan Line*
**35029* Ellerman Lines*
**35030* Elder-Dempster Lines*

(1) At first named Blue Funnel Line, later became Blue Funnel Certum Pete Finem

4–6–2 Class WC BR class 7P5F 'West Country' *(see pages 44 and 90*)*

*21C101 *(34001)* Exeter
21C102 *(34002)* Salisbury
*21C103 *(34003)* Plymouth
*21C104 *(34004)* Yeovil
*21C105 *(34005)* Barnstaple
21C106 *(34006)* Bude
21C107 *(34007)* Wadebridge
*21C108 *(34008)* Padstow
*21C109 *(34009)* Lyme Regis
*21C110 *(34010)* Sidmouth
21C111 *(34011)* Tavistock
*21C112 *(34012)* Launceston
*21C113 *(34013)* Okehampton
*21C114 *(34014)* Budleigh Salterton
21C115 *(34015)* Exmouth
*21C116 *(34016)* Bodmin
*21C117 *(34017)* Ilfracombe
*21C118 *(34018)* Axminster
21C119 *(34019)* Bideford
21C120 *(34020)* Seaton
*21C121 *(34021)* Dartmoor
*21C122 *(34022)* Exmoor
21C123 *(34023)* Blackmore Vale (2)
*21C124 *(34024)* Tamar Valley
*21C125 *(34025)* Whimple (3)
*21C126 *(34026)* Yes Tor
*21C127 *(34027)* Taw Valley
*21C128 *(34028)* Eddystone
*21C129 *(34029)* Lundy
21C130 *(34030)* Watersmeet
*21C131 *(34031)* Torrington
*21C132 *(34032)* Camelford
21C133 *(34033)* Chard
*21C134 *(34034)* Honiton
21C135 *(34035)* Shaftesbury
*21C136 *(34036)* Westward Ho
*21C137 *(34037)* Clovelly
21C138 *(34038)* Lynton
*21C139 *(34039)* Boscastle
*21C140 *(34040)* Crewkerne
21C141 *(34041)* Wilton
*21C142 *(34042)* Dorchester
21C143 *(34043)* Combe Martin

*21C144 *(34044)* Woolacombe
*21C145 *(34045)* Ottery St. Mary
*21C146 *(34046)* Braunton
*21C147 *(34047)* Callington
*21C148 *(34048)* Crediton

 34091 *Weymouth*
 34092 *City of Wells (4)*
*34093 *Saunton*
 34094 *Mortehoe*
*34095 *Brentor*
*34096 *Trevone*
*34097 *Holsworthy*
*34098 *Templecombe*
 34099 *Lynmouth*
*34100 *Appledore*
*34101 *Hartland*
 34102 *Lapford*
 34103 *Calstock*
*34104 *Bere Alston*
 34105 *Swanage*
 34106 *Lydford*
 34107 *Blandford Forum (5)*
*34108 *Wincanton*

(2) At first named 'Blackmoor Vale'; altered in 1950
(3) No 21C125 'Whimple' was at first named 'Rough Tor' (for a few days only).
(4) Named 'Wells' until November 1949.
(5) Named 'Blandford' until October 1952.

4–6–2 Class BB BR class 7P5F 'Battle of Britain' (see pages 56 and 90)*

 21C149 *(34049)* Anti-Aircraft Command
*21C150 *(34050)* Royal Observer Corps

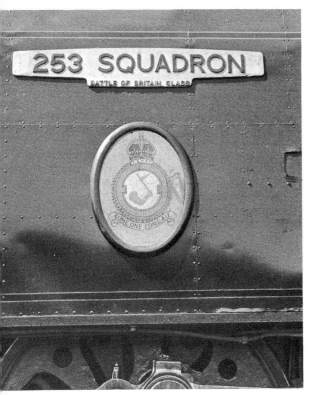

Above left:
Left hand nameplate of 'Merchant Navy' Pacific No 21C3 (35003) *Royal Mail*, in original state with the engine finished in matt Malachite green, with yellow lining. *Author's collection*

Left:
'Battle of Britain' class No 34084 *253 Squadron*, in unmodified form, with Brunswick green livery and orange and black lining. Sandbox fillers located each side of the decorative oval enamel plaque. *D. H. Cape*

21C151 *(34051)* Winston Churchill
*21C152 *(34052)* Lord Dowding
*21C153 *(34053)* Sir Keith Park
21C154 *(34054)* Lord Beaverbrook
21C155 *(34055)* Fighter Pilot
*21C156 *(34056)* Croydon
21C157 *(34057)* Biggin Hill
*21C158 *(34058)* Sir Frederick Pile
*21C159 *(34059)* Sir Archibald Sinclair
*21C160 *(34060)* 25 Squadron
21C161 *(34061)* 73 Squadron
*21C162 *(34062)* 17 Squadron
21C163 *(34063)* 229 Squadron
21C164 *(34064)* Fighter Command
21C165 *(34065)* Hurricane
21C166 *(34066)* Spitfire
21C167 *(34067)* Tangmere
21C168 *(34068)* Kenley
21C169 *(34069)* Hawkinge
21C170 *(34070)* Manston
34071 601 Squadron (6)
34072 257 Squadron
34073 249 Squadron
34074 46 Squadron
34075 264 Squadron
34076 41 Squadron
**34077 603 Squadron*
34078 222 Squadron
34079 141 Squadron
34080 74 Squadron
34081 92 Squadron
**34082 615 Squadron*
34083 605 Squadron
34084 253 Squadron
**34085 501 Squadron*
34086 219 Squadron
**34087 145 Squadron*
**34088 213 Squadron*
**34089 602 Squadron*
**34090 Sir Eustace Missenden, Southern*
Railway
**34109 Sir Trafford Leigh-Mallory*
34110 66 Squadron

Above:
Right hand nameplate of 'West Country' class Pacific
No 34003, after conversation, with the plates
supported by a backplate (see page 94). In the
unmodified form, the decorative plaque was located
below the nameplate. *Author's collection*

Right:
Restored 'West Country' Pacific No 34092 *City of Wells*
darkens the sky as it lifts the empty coaching stock of a
Pullman special, on the Keighley & Worth Valley
Railway, over Keighley bank summit on 21 April 1982.
The ex SR freight vans to the left of the locomotive are
in fact in an adjacent siding, and not attached to the
train; despite appearances! *David Olsen-Hopper*

*(6) Carried the name '615 Squadron' for a short
period in 1948.*

The 'Leader' class 0-6-6-0T design (see page
66) was intended to carry names, but did not
survive long enough for such adornment. The
original Bulleid notation would have been Nos
CC101-105 and names known to have been
selected by Bulleid himself for the first two
were *Missenden* and *Churchill,* although these
were actually carried by 'Battle of Britain' class
engines in slightly different form.

Appendix 4

Preserved Locomotives

I wrote the first edition of this book in the early 1970s, when Bulleid's locomotives, those still extant that is to say, were mostly to be found rusting away in a South Wales scrapyard. The memories of BR main line running was however still fairly fresh on my mind, and happily a handful of preservation schemes had already got under way in an attempt to keep at least a few *static* examples for the future; unless homes could be found for them to run in steam. For some years BR had been very anti-steam, and a complete ban had existed on the use of steam locomotives over their routes. Not in my wildest dreams did I foresee the possibility of once again witnessing Bulleid's locomotives hauling revenue-earning passenger trains over BR routes — and yet exactly that has since come about! Moreover, if anyone had suggested to me then, that in 1984 there would still be 32 Bulleid locomotives in existence, and some of

Below:
When the first edition of this book was published the Barry scrapyard was full of Bulleid Pacifics forlornly awaiting cutting-up. Scenes such as this, where rebuilt 'West Country' No 34101 *Hartland* (on the left) and un-rebuilt 'West Country' No 34105 *Swanage* are seen awaiting the torch, were abundant. Both locomotives have since been rescued. *D. L. Percival*

Right:
The rescue by a group of enthusiasts and subsequent restoration of rebuilt 'Merchant Navy' class Pacific No 35028 *Clan Line* demonstrated what *could* be done with sheer enthusiasm as the prime-mover, and the locomotive certainly presented a challenge both to their financial resources and physical labour! No 35028 makes a beautiful picture, posed with 'Cumbrian Coast Express' headboard, on 29 May 1979. *J. H. Cooper-Smith*

Bottom right:
Replica 'Golden Arrow' headboard and flags (minus the arrows on the smoke-deflectors, however), grace the front end of No 35028 *Clan Line* – a vivid reminder of bygone days at Stewarts Lane depot! *J. Harvey*

Left:
The permission for a return to steam on BR, after a period of total ban, gave fresh impetus to the various preservation schemes, and sights such as this – as No 35028 *Clan Line* slips whilst backing-down onto a Merchant Navy Locomotive Preservation Society Railtour special, at Stratford-Upon-Avon on 26 October 1974 – gave a new generation of enthusiasts their first real taste of what steam traction was all about. *John R. Woolley*

Below:
Photographed on the same day as the previous picture, No 35028 *Clan Line* heads the return special out of Stratford-Upon-Avon, near Bishopton; en route to Didcot. The play of exhaust around the chimney base was a feature of the rebuilt versions of both the 'Merchant Navy' class and the Light Pacifics, under certain working conditions, (see also page 93). *R. E. B. Siviter*

Top right:
Keeping a preserved locomotive in full working order, in particular if it is to work over BR metals is a major task, and it has been further complicated by the need to remove certain items, (such as blue asbestos boiler cladding), or to improve certain items, to meet stringent BR requirements. Here, the boiler and firebox of *Clan Line* are stripped of blue asbestos, and the cab itself has been temporarily moved back some 3ft to improve access to the firebox area. Photographed on 26 May 1981. *J. Harvey*

Below:
Looking rather like an 'Austerity' wartime version of the 'Merchant Navy' Pacific, (in fact, such an idea *was* once envisaged by Bulleid himself!) No 35005 *Canadian Pacific* is seen in the open air at Carnforth on 17 February 1979; after restoration work had begun. *Brian Morrison*

Bottom:
By the time this picture of No 35005 *Canadian Pacific* was taken, inside Carnforth shed on 25 August 1980, the locomotive had been drastically denuded and was minus boiler, cab, and leading coupled wheels. It is doubtful if BR would have even contemplated such a complete overhaul during their final years of ownership of the 'Merchant Navy' rebuilds, in view of the costs involved, and the time taken! *Peter Harris*

them in full working order at that – I would have pronounced them to be delirious beyond question! Now I must eat humble pie.

The efforts which have been made by railway enthusiasts seem to compare with such feats as building the Great Wall of China. Coming from all professions and stratas of society, and all age groups, they have united to rescue Britain's steam locomotive heritage and high on the list of the locomotives they have saved are those of O. V. S. Bulleid – albeit in many cases in their late, rebuilt, BR form. To all these enthusiasts and their devotion, we owe a very great deal indeed.

A curious coincidence came to light (too late to be included) whilst I was working on the original version of this book. At the time I was living in a fairly remote habitation on the upper-most slopes of Box Hill, near Dorking in Surrey. This natural beauty spot, of chalk formation, and with an abundance of protected flora and fauna, (the National Trust has Box Hill in its care), overlooks the valley of the River Mole, where nestles the town of Dorking, and adjacent, Deepdene. I already knew that Deepdene (in prewar days a quality hotel), had

been the wartime headquarters of the Southern Railway and whilst writing my mind often went to those difficult years, when Bulleid had been in charge of SR motive power affairs, and I tried to visualise the sorts of problems that had confronted him – leading for example to the design and construction of the Class Q1 0-6-0s, and to his perseverence with the teething troubles of the 'Merchant Navy' Pacifics. Sometimes when looking down the hill my eye was caught by a large house called 'Boxhurst' nestling amidst pine trees in a sheltered fold of the hill, not far from the winding River Mole. It was, I used to think, a rather appealing place to live. Imagine my astonishment when, having completed the manuscript, I paid a visit to Bulleid's eldest son, living in Sussex, (who had kindly consented to write the Foreword to the book), and was told that the house I so admired was one and the same that the Bulleid family had lived in since November 1937 and all during the war!

I particularly liked a story H. A. V. Bulleid told me about the day someone in authority along the Redhill–Reading (ex SECR) line – which passes close to 'Boxhurst' telephoned the

Left:
One 'Merchant Navy' Pacific was quite deliberately cut-up – or more accurately – *sectioned*! No 35029 *Ellerman Lines* was rescued and restored as a static exhibit for the National Railway Museum. One half of the locomotive was cut to expose the innards, in brilliant fashion, with each portion – firebox, boiler, smokebox, cylinders, etc – easily understood by the visitors, and with an electrical drive to the coupled wheels to show them in motion. No 35029 is housed at York and is a ceaseless attraction to all who visit the museum.
Crown Copyright/National Railway Museum

Below:
As more and more locomotives were rescued from Barry, scenes such as this became quite a feature of the roads! Here is No 35027 *Port Line* at the junction of the A473 and the M4 near Bridgend (intersection 35), ready to head east on 18 December 1982 to its new home on the Swindon & Cricklade Railway.
W. S. Trite

Below:
The picture speaks for itself! No 35018 *British India Line* had arrived at the Mid Hants Railway, (the 'Watercress Line') where restoration awaited it, eventually to make it a fitting companion to restored rebuilt 'West Country' No 34016 *Bodmin*, (pictured in the background) at Alresford station. *Mid Hants*

Top:
Steamtown, Carnforth, 8.45am on 28 November 1981, and 'West Country' Pacific No 34092 *City of Wells* is being prepared for a main line duty. In the background is ex LNER Gresley Class A4 Pacific No 4498 *Sir Nigel*

Gresley, also in steam. No 34092 is restored to the latterday BR condition, with cut-down tender and Brunswick green livery; BR AWS is fitted.
Graham Wignall

Below left:
The Bluebell Railway's restored 'West Country' makes an interesting contrast to *City of Wells* because it has been returned to earlier Southern Railway condition, with Malachite green livery and original style tender. No 21C123 *Blackmore Vale* even has the small smoke deflectors of the original design – only the cab, with its angled windows betrays a latter-day modification to Bulleid's original conception. The picture was taken on 14 June 1981 as *Blackmore Vale* headed for Horsted Keynes on the 16.42 from Sheffield Park; near Freshfield Halt. *Ramona Sharman*

Above:
The Keighley & Worth Valley Railway's restored 'West Country' class 4-6-2 No 34092 *City of Wells* is seen here arriving at Oakworth with a late afternoon train for Oxenhope in August 1980, in true 'stopping-train' style. *John Sagar*

Right:
Much more glamorous is the spectacle of *City of Wells* pounding along with a 'Golden Arrow' special working in a snowbound landscape; passing Wennington Junction signalbox on 12 December 1981. Such images do indeed recall the heyday of the Bulleid Pacifics in BR service, when snowy days in Kent could provide very trying conditions for the enginemen. *A. R. Cocklin*

Bulleid household to tell them that the first of his new 'Austerity' class Q1 0-6-0s No C1 was due to travel past the house. Everyone at 'Boxhurst' turned-out to see the gaunt new machine steam by in due course. When he told me that story, neither of us could imagine that the very same locomotive, as BR No 33001, would once again power passenger trains, as it nowadays does on the Bluebell Railway.

The interest in Bulleid and his locomotives has steadily increased over the years since his death, and H. A. V. Bulleid's own book *Bulleid of the Southern* published by Ian Allan Ltd in 1977, at last revealed a lot of the secrets surrounding development of the Pacifics, and the revolutionary 'Leader' class; whilst also giving us a true insight into the life, times and personality of this most brilliant of Chief Mechanical Engineers. I have added this Appendix to my own book as an acknowledgement of the progress made since 1977, in which year the first edition appeared in print, and in which I listed 9 locomotives as preserved – compared to today's staggering total of 32.

Perhaps the most impressive aspect of this preservation progress is that it has in many

cases been carried out in working conditions that would soon have the trade union officials, (which mercifully do not exist in railway preservation circles!) demanding a 'down tools' protest. Locomotives have been dismantled, stripped of rusty parts, cleaned, repaired, laboriously put back together, undercoated,

Left:
Return to steam on the 'Watercress Line' for rebuilt 'West Country' No 34016 *Bodmin*, seen in sylvan surroundings, leaving Alresford on the 11.30am to Ropley on 18 July 1982. It is difficult to visualise that this superb machine was for a long time lying rusty and neglected in a scrapyard before being rescued and so brilliantly restored to life! *J. H. Cooper-Smith*

Top:
Restoration work was well advanced when this picture of No 34016 *Bodmin* was taken, and it shows the sort of working conditions that were then available! *Mid Hants*

Above:
The finishing touch; superbly executed! *L. G. Tilbury*

painted and varnished, quite often in the open air, and in all weathers; sometimes with just sheets of polythene or tarpaulins for protective cover. Moreover most of the work has taken place at weekends, or in leisure periods.

Another problem has been to recover or replace many missing bits and pieces, or to make new ones from patterns. Most of the Bulleid locomotives suffered from vandalism when lying idle, and brass and copper were high on the list for removal. Added to this, some parts – such as cab windows and electric lights – were inviting targets for small boys with stones. Nature also played its destructive role, with corrosion of the more prone metal areas, particularly cab side sheets and roofs and the air-smoothed casings of the un-rebuilt engines.

Once having secured *their* particular prize from Barry, then the fun really began!

I have decided to list the preserved Pacific locomotives by class, commencing with those still basically in Bulleid condition. As some are still in Barry (reserved) and some are stored away, it is not practical to describe the present-day condition of each individual locomotive. Quite a few are in the lengthy throes of reconstruction, others still await their turn. Needless to say finance is a problem, as well as labour resources, and it may well be another decade before the full Bulleid fleet is restored to its former splendour. A sobering thought is that enough 'Pacifics' have been rescued to take over the day-to-day operations of at least one area of todays BR main 'InterCity' routes – should all else fail!

Running a restored steam engine over BR

tracks, or on the private railways, entails high safety standards, and each locomotive has to be inspected and passed as fit at specific intervals. Boilers, wheel flanges and tyre thickness, and other important details have to be maintained to specification. Thus, once restored, the labour of love is by no means over! Other factors, such as the removal of blue asbestos boiler insulation have to be considered either during restoration work, or (as in the case of No 35028), at a later stage. One must fervently hope that the fires of enthusiasm will not diminish, because if they were to do so – then so would the fires that are kindled in the fireboxes of the restored Bulleid locomotives.

Right:
Bodmin again, and what a magnificent restoration job was achieved! No locomotive outshopped by Eastleigh in BR steam days excelled this standard of finish – achieved by enthusiastic labour. Photograph taken at Ropley on 17 July 1982.   *J. H. Cooper-Smith*

Below:
Rebuilt 'West Country' Pacific No 34039 *Boscastle* stands naked in the open air at Loughborough, on the Great Central Railway on 15 July 1974, with the front end, frames, smokebox saddle and cylinders, and firebox already protected against corrosion.
Graham F. Scott-Lowe

Unrebuilt 'West Country' class 4-6-2

No	Name	Usual location/Railway	Status
34007	*Wadebridge*	Bodmin	Restoration
34023	*Blackmoor Vale*	Bluebell	Overhaul
34092	*City of Wells*	Keighley & Worth Valley	Overhaul
34105	*Swanage*	Mid-Hants	Operational

Unrebuilt 'Battle of Britain' class 4-6-2

No	Name	Usual location/Railway	Status
34051	*Winston Churchill* †	National Railway Museum, York	Museum
34067	*Tangmere*	Mid-Hants	Restoration
34070	*Manston*	Richboro Power Station (P)	Restoration
34072	*257 Squadron*	Swanage	Operational
34073	*249 Squadron*	Brighton (P)	Restoration
34081	*92 Squadron*	Nene Valley	Restoration

Rebuilt 'West Country' class 4-6-2

No	Name	Usual location/Railway	Status
34010	*Sidmouth*	Teesside (P)	Restoration
34016	*Bodmin*	Mid-Hants	Overhaul
34027	*Taw Valley*	Severn Valley	Operational
34028	*Eddystone*	Sellindge	Restoration
34039	*Boscastle*	Great Central	Operational
34046	*Braunton*	Brighton (P)	Stored
34101	*Hartland*	Great Central	Restoration

Rebuilt 'Battle of Britain' class 4-6-2

No	Name	Usual location/Railway	Status
34053	*Sir Keith Park*	Railway Age, Crewe	Restoration
34058	*Sir Frederick Pile*	Avon Valley	Restoration
34059	*Sir Archibald Sinclair*	Bluebell	Restoration

Rebuilt 'Merchant Navy' class 4-6-2

No	Name	Usual location/Railway	Status
35005	*Canadian Pacific*	Great Central	Operational
35006	*Peninsular & Oriental S. N. Co*	Gloucestershire-Warwickshire	Restoration
35009	*Shaw Savill*	Brighton (P)	Stored
35010	*Blue Star*	North Woolwich (P)	Restoration
35011	*General Steam Navigation*	Brighton (P)	Stored
35018	*British India Line*	Mid-Hants	Restoration
35022	*Holland-America Line*	Swanage	Stored
35025	*Brocklebank Line*	Great Central	Restoration
35027	*Port Line*	Bluebell	Operational
35028	*Clan Line*	Southall (P)	Overhaul
35029	*Ellerman Lines* *†	National Railway Museum, York	Sectioned

'Austerity' 'Q1' class 0-6-0

No	Name	Usual location/Railway	Status
33001	—	Bluebell†	Operational

(P) Locomotive situated on a private site   * Sectioned exhibit
† Owned by National Railway Museum   Stored indicates locomotive awaiting restoration

Right:
By the time this picture was taken, on 10 April 1982, work on *Boscastle* at Loughborough had reached quite an advanced stage; although there was clearly much still to be done before she could proudly steam once more on the Great Central Railway.   *Graham Wignall*

Below:
No doubt quite a few motorists were fuming at the delay, as rebuilt 'Battle of Britain' Class No 34059 *Sir Archibald Sinclair* is hauled through Arundel, Sussex en route to its new home on the Bluebell Railway on 27 October 1979.   *J. G. Mallinson*

Right:
Happily an example of Bulleid's wartime class Q1
0-6-0s, No 33001 was selected for official preservation,
and restored to working order. The locomotive is on
loan to the Bluebell Railway, and is seen here at
Sheffield Park about to leave on an afternoon working
to Horsted Keynes on 23 October 1982.
Colin J. Marsden

Below:
What more fitting picture could exist to end this review
of preserved Bulleid locomotives than this
double-headed Bluebell Railway train? Bulleid himself
would have been proud to see the excellent
restoration work achieved on both locomotives; which
portray his designs to perfection. Class Q1 0-6-0 No
33001 assists 'West Country' Pacific No 34023
Blackmore Vale on the 3.55pm from Sheffield Park on
14 September 1980; seen just after leaving Sheffield
Park. *Brian Stephenson*

Bibliography

Reference was made to the following books and periodicals whilst compiling this Pictorial History. The reader seeking further information on O. V. S. Bulleid, his life and his locomotives, is recommended to them:

Bulleid, H. A. V. *Master Builders of Steam.* Ian Allan Ltd.
Day-Lewis, S. *Bulleid – Last Giant of Steam.* George Allen & Unwin.
Nock, O. S. *Southern Steam.* David & Charles.
Allen, Cecil J. and Townroe, S.C. *Bulleid Pacifics of the Southern Railway.* Ian Allan Ltd.
Reed, Brian *Merchant Navy Pacifics Loco-Profile No. 22* Profile Publications
Rowledge, J. W. P. *The Turf Burner. Ireland's last steam locomotive design.* Irish Railway Record Society.
Winkworth, D. W. *Bulleid's Pacifics* George Allen & Unwin.

Various issues of the following periodicals and journals:

The Locomotive
Trains Illustrated/Modern Railways.
Railway Gazette
Railway Magazine
Railway World
Railway Observer (RCTS)
SLS Journal

Below:
With a Stanier LMSR tender attached. 'Merchant Navy' class Pacific No 35017 *Belgian Marine* storms out of Hadley North Tunnel on an ER Kings Cross-Leeds train in May 1948, during the historic Exchange trials.
Rev. B. Whitworth